SECOND EDITION

Data Structures and Algorithms in Javascript

Michael McMillan

Beijing · Boston · Farnham · Sebastopol · Tokyo

Data Structures and Algorithms with JavaScript

by Michael McMillan

Printed in the United States of America.

Published by O'Reilly Media, Inc., 1005 Gravenstein Highway North, Sebastopol, CA 95472.

O'Reilly books may be purchased for educational, business, or sales promotional use. Online editions are also available for most titles (*http://safaribooksonline.com*). For more information, contact our corporate/institutional sales department: 800-998-9938 or *corporate@oreilly.com*.

Editors: Brian MacDonald and Meghan Blanchette
Production Editor: Melanie Yarbrough
Copyeditor: Becca Freed
Proofreader: Amanda Kersey

Indexer: Ellen Troutman-Zaig
Interior Designer: David Futato
Cover Designer: Ellie Volkhausen
Illustrator: Rebecca Demarest

March 2014:   First Edition

Revision History for the First Edition
2014-03-06:   First Release
2015-10-21:   Second Release

See *http://oreilly.com/catalog/errata.csp?isbn=9781449364939* for release details.

978-1-449-36493-9

[LSI]

Table of Contents

Preface

Over the past few years, JavaScript has been used more and more as a server-side computer programming language owing to platforms such as Node.js and Spider-Monkey. Now that JavaScript programming is moving out of the browser, programmers will find they need to use many of the tools provided by more conventional languages, such as C++ and Java. Among these tools are classic data structures such as linked lists, stacks, queues, and graphs, as well as classic algorithms for sorting and searching data. This book discusses how to implement these data structures and algorithms for server-side JavaScript programming.

JavaScript programmers will find this book useful because it discusses how to implement data structures and algorithms within the constraints that JavaScript places them, such as arrays that are really objects, overly global variables, and a prototype-based object system. JavaScript has an unfair reputation as a "bad" programming language, but this book demonstrates how you can use JavaScript to develop efficient and effective data structures and algorithms using the language's "good parts."

Why Study Data Structures and Algorithms

I am assuming that many of you reading this book do not have a formal education in computer science. If you do, then you already know why studying data structures and algorithms is important. If you do not have a degree in computer science or haven't studied these topics formally, you should read this section.

The computer scientist Nicklaus Wirth wrote a computer programming textbook titled *Algorithms + Data Structures = Programs* (Prentice-Hall). That title is the essence of computer programming. Any computer program that goes beyond the trivial "Hello, world!" will usually require some type of structure to manage the data the program is written to manipulate, along with one or more algorithms for translating the data from its input form to its output form.

For many programmers who didn't study computer science in school, the only data structure they are familiar with is the array. Arrays are great for some problems, but for many complex problems, they are simply not sophisticated enough. Most experienced programmers will admit that for many programming problems, once they come up with the proper data structure, the algorithms needed to solve the problem are easier to design and implement.

An example of a data structure that leads to efficient algorithms is the binary search tree (BST). A binary search tree is designed so that it is easy to find the minimum and maximum values of a set of data, yielding an algorithm that is more efficient than the best search algorithms available. Programmers unfamiliar with BSTs will instead probably use a simpler data structure that ends up being less efficient.

Studying algorithms is important because there is always more than one algorithm that can be used to solve a problem, and knowing which ones are the most efficient is important for the productive programmer. For example, there are at least six or seven ways to sort a list of data, but knowing that the Quicksort algorithm is more efficient than the selection sort algorithm will lead to a much more efficient sorting process. Or that it's fairly easy to implement a sequential or linear search algorithm for a list of data, but knowing that the binary sort algorithm can sometimes be twice as efficient as the sequential search will lead to a better program.

The comprehensive study of data structures and algorithms teaches you not only which data structures and which algorithms are the most efficient, but you also learn how to decide which data structures and which algorithms are the most appropriate for the problem at hand. There will often be trade-offs involved when writing a program, especially in the JavaScript environment, and knowing the ins and outs of the various data structures and algorithms covered in this book will help you make the proper decision for any particular programming problem you are trying to solve.

What You Need for This Book

The programming environment we use in this book is the JavaScript shell based on the SpiderMonkey JavaScript engine. Chapter 1 provides instructions on downloading the shell for your environment. Other shells will work as well, such as the Node.js JavaScript shell, though you will have to make some translations for the programs in the book to work in Node. Other than the shell, the only thing you need is a text editor for writing your JavaScript programs.

Organization of the Book

- Chapter 1 presents an overview of the JavaScript language, or at least the features of the JavaScript language used in this book. This chapter also demonstrates through use the programming style used throughout the other chapters.

- Chapter 2 discusses the most common data structure in computer programming: the array, which is native to JavaScript.

- Chapter 3 introduces the first implemented data structure: the list.

- Chapter 4 covers the stack data structure. Stacks are used throughout computer science in both compiler and operating system implementations.

- Chapter 5 discusses queue data structures. Queues are an abstraction of the lines you stand in at a bank or the grocery store. Queues are used extensively in simulation software where data has to be lined up before it is processed.

- Chapter 6 covers Linked lists. A linked list is a modification of the list data structure, where each element is a separate object linked to the objects on either side of it. Linked lists are efficient when you need to perform multiple insertions and deletions in your program.

- Chapter 7 demonstrates how to build and use dictionaries, which are data structures that store data as key-value pairs.

- One way to implement a dictionary is to use a hash table, and Chapter 8 discusses how to build hash tables and the hash algorithms that are used to store data in the table.

- Chapter 9 covers the set data structure. Sets are often not covered in data structure books, but they can be useful for storing data that is not supposed to have duplicates in the data set.

- Binary trees and binary search trees are the subject of Chapter 10. As mentioned earlier, binary search trees are useful for storing data that needs to be stored originally in sorted form.

- Chapter 11 covers graphs and graph algorithms. Graphs are used to represent data such as the nodes of a computer network or the cities on a map.

- Chapter 12 moves from data structures to algorithms and discusses various algorithms for sorting data, including both simple sorting algorithms that are easy to implement but are not efficient for large data sets, and more complex algorithms that are appropriate for larger data sets.

- Chapter 13 also covers algorithms, this time searching algorithms such as sequential search and binary search.

- The last chapter of the book, Chapter 14, discusses a couple more advanced algorithms for working with data—dynamic programming and greedy algorithms. These algorithms are useful for solving hard problems where a more traditional algorithm is either too slow or too hard to implement. We examine some classic problems for both dynamic programming and greedy algorithms in the chapter.

Conventions Used in This Book

The following typographical conventions are used in this book:

Italic
> Indicates new terms, URLs, email addresses, filenames, and file extensions.

`Constant width`
> Used for program listings, as well as within paragraphs to refer to program elements such as variable or function names, databases, data types, environment variables, statements, and keywords.

`Constant width bold`
> Shows commands or other text that should be typed literally by the user.

`Constant width italic`
> Shows text that should be replaced with user-supplied values or by values determined by context.

Using Code Examples

Supplemental material (code examples, exercises, etc.) is available for download at *https://github.com/oreillymedia/data_structures_and_algorithms_using_javascript*.

This book is here to help you get your job done. In general, if example code is offered with this book, you may use it in your programs and documentation. You do not need to contact us for permission unless you're reproducing a significant portion of the code. For example, writing a program that uses several chunks of code from this book does not require permission. Selling or distributing a CD-ROM of examples from O'Reilly books does require permission. Answering a question by citing this book and quoting example code does not require permission. Incorporating a significant amount of example code from this book into your product's documentation does require permission.

We appreciate, but do not require, attribution. An attribution usually includes the title, author, publisher, and ISBN. For example: "*Data Structures and Algorithms Using JavaScript* by Michael McMillian (O'Reilly). Copyright 2014 Michael McMillan, 978-1-449-36493-9."

If you feel your use of code examples falls outside fair use or the permission given above, feel free to contact us at *permissions@oreilly.com*.

Safari® Books Online

 *Safari Books Online* is an on-demand digital library that delivers expert content in both book and video form from the world's leading authors in technology and business.

Technology professionals, software developers, web designers, and business and creative professionals use Safari Books Online as their primary resource for research, problem solving, learning, and certification training.

Safari Books Online offers a range of plans and pricing for enterprise, government, education, and individuals.

Members have access to thousands of books, training videos, and prepublication manuscripts in one fully searchable database from publishers like O'Reilly Media, Prentice Hall Professional, Addison-Wesley Professional, Microsoft Press, Sams, Que, Peachpit Press, Focal Press, Cisco Press, John Wiley & Sons, Syngress, Morgan Kaufmann, IBM Redbooks, Packt, Adobe Press, FT Press, Apress, Manning, New Riders, McGraw-Hill, Jones & Bartlett, Course Technology, and hundreds more. For more information about Safari Books Online, please visit us online.

How to Contact Us

Please address comments and questions concerning this book to the publisher:

O'Reilly Media, Inc.
1005 Gravenstein Highway North
Sebastopol, CA 95472
800-998-9938 (in the United States or Canada)
707-829-0515 (international or local)
707-829-0104 (fax)

We have a web page for this book, where we list errata, examples, and any additional information. You can access this page at *http://bit.ly/data-structures-and-algorithms-js*.

To comment or ask technical questions about this book, send email to *bookquestions@oreilly.com*.

For more information about our books, courses, conferences, and news, see our website at *http://www.oreilly.com*.

Find us on Facebook: *http://facebook.com/oreilly*

Follow us on Twitter: *http://twitter.com/oreillymedia*

Watch us on YouTube: *http://www.youtube.com/oreillymedia*

Content Updates

October 20, 2015

- Fixed typos, ambiguities, and other issues regarding clarity
- Removed the iterative version of Mergesort and replaced it with a recursive one
- Cleaned up and reorganized the repo; all code from the book is now there, and keyed to text
- Added parallel repo of all the code modified to run with Node

Acknowledgments

There are always lots of people to thank when you've finished writing a book. I'd like to thank my acquisition editor, Simon St. Laurent, for believing in this book and getting me started writing it. Meghan Blanchette worked hard to keep me on schedule, and if I went off schedule, it definitely wasn't her fault. Brian MacDonald worked extremely hard to make this book as understandable as possible, and he helped make several parts of the text much clearer than I had written them originally. I also want to thank my technical reviewers for reading all the text as well as the code, and for pointing out places where both my prose and my code needed to be clearer. My colleague and illustrator, Cynthia Fehrenbach, did an outstanding job translating my chicken scratchings into crisp, clear illustrations, and she deserves extra praise for her willingness to redraw several illustrations at the very last minute. Finally, I'd like to thank all the people at Mozilla for designing an excellent JavaScript engine and shell and writing some excellent documentation for using both the language and the shell.

CHAPTER 1

The JavaScript Programming Environment and Model

This chapter describes the JavaScript programming environment and the programming constructs we'll use in this book to define the various data structures and algorithms examined.

The JavaScript Environment

JavaScript has historically been a programming language that ran only inside a web browser. However, in the past few years, there has been the development of JavaScript programming environments that can be run from the desktop, or similarly, from a server. In this book we use one such environment: the JavaScript shell that is part of Mozilla's comprehensive JavaScript environment known as SpiderMonkey.

To download the JavaScript shell, navigate to the Nightly Build web page (*http://mzl.la/MKOuFY*). Scroll to the bottom of the page and pick the download that matches your computer system.

Once you've downloaded the program, you have two choices for using the shell. You can use it either in interactive mode or to interpret JavaScript programs stored in a file. To use the shell in interactive mode, type the command js at a command prompt. The shell prompt, js>, will appear and you are ready to start entering JavaScript expressions and statements.

The following is a typical interaction with the shell:

```
js> 1
1
js> 1+2
3
```

```
js> var num = 1;
js> num*124
124
js> for (var i = 1; i < 6; ++i) {
    print(i);
}
1
2
3
4
5
js>
```

You can enter arithmetic expressions and the shell will immediately evaluate them. You can write any legal JavaScript statement and the shell will immediately evaluate it as well. The interactive shell is great for exploring JavaScript statements to discover how they work. To leave the shell when you are finished, type the command quit().

The other way to use the shell is to have it interpret complete JavaScript programs. This is how we will use the shell throughout the rest of the book.

To use the shell to intepret programs, you first have to create a file that contains a JavaScript program. You can use any text editor, making sure you save the file as plain text. The only requirement is that the file must have a *.js* extension. The shell has to see this extension to know the file is a JavaScript program.

Once you have your file saved, you interpret it by typing the js command followed by the full filename of your program. For example, if you saved the for loop code fragment that's shown earlier in a file named *loop.js*, you would enter the following:

```
c:\js>js loop.js
```

which would produce the following output:

```
1
2
3
4
5
```

After the program is executed, control is returned to the command prompt.

JavaScript Programming Practices

In this section we discuss how we use JavaScript. We realize that programmers have different styles and practices when it comes to writing programs, and we want to describe ours here at the beginning of the book so that you'll understand the more complex code we present in the rest of the book. This isn't a tutorial on using JavaScript but is just a guide to how we use the fundamental constructs of the language.

Declaring and Initializing Variables

JavaScript variables declared outside of a function are global by default and, strictly speaking, don't have to be declared before using. When a JavaScript variable is initialized without first being declared, using the var keyword, it becomes a global variable. In this book, however, we follow the convention used with compiled languages such as C++ and Java by declaring all variables before their first use. The added benefit to doing this is that variables declared within function are created as local variables. We will talk more about variable scope later in this chapter.

You can use *strict mode* to ensure variables are declared before use. Insert the following line *exactly* before any other statement:

```
'use strict';
```

Or

```
"use strict";
```

To declare a variable in JavaScript, use the keyword var followed by a variable name, and optionally, an assignment expression. Here are some examples:

```
var number;
var name;
var rate = 1.2;
var greeting = "Hello, world!";
var flag = false;
```

Arithmetic and Math Library Functions in JavaScript

JavaScript utilizes the standard arithmetic operators:

- + (addition)
- - (subtraction)
- * (multiplication)
- / (division)
- % (modulo)

JavaScript also has a math library you can use for advanced functions such as square root, absolute value, and the trigonometric functions. The arithmetic operators follow the standard order of operations, and parentheses can be used to modify that order.

Example 1-1 shows some examples of performing arithmetic in JavaScript, as well as examples of using several of the mathematical functions.

Example 1-1. Arithmetic and math functions in JavaScript

```
var x = 3;
var y = 1.1;
print(x + y);
print(x * y);
print((x+y)*(x-y));
var z = 9;
print(Math.sqrt(z));
print(Math.abs(y/x));
```

The output from this program is:

```
4.1
3.3000000000000003
7.789999999999999
3
0.3666666666666667
```

If you don't want or need the precision shown above, you can format a number to a fixed precision:

```
var x = 3;
var y = 1.1;
var z = x * y;
print(z.toFixed(2)); // displays 3.30
```

Decision Constructs

Decision constructs allow our programs to make decisions on what programming statements to execute based on a Boolean expression. The two decision constructs we use in this book are the if statement and the switch statement.

The if statement comes in three forms:

- The simple if statement
- The if-else statement
- The if-else if statement

Example 1-2 shows how to write a simple if statement.

Example 1-2. The simple if statement

```
var mid = 25;
var high = 50;
var low = 1;
var current = 13;
var found = -1;
if (current < mid) {
```

```
    mid = (current-low) / 2;
}
```

Example 1-3 demonstrates the `if-else` statement.

Example 1-3. The `if-else` statement

```
var mid = 25;
var high = 50;
var low = 1;
var current = 13;
var found = -1;
if (current < mid) {
    mid = (current-low) / 2;
} else {
    mid = (current+high) / 2;
}
```

Example 1-4 illustrates the `if-else if` statement.

Example 1-4. The `if-else if` statement

```
var mid = 25;
var high = 50;
var low = 1;
var current = 13;
var found = -1;
if (current < mid) {
    mid = (current-low) / 2;
}
else if (current > mid) {
    mid = (current+high) / 2;
}
else {
    found = current;
}
```

The other decision structure we use in this book is the `switch` statement. This statement provides a cleaner, more structured construction when you there's a set of simple decisions. Example 1-5 demonstrates how the `switch` statement works.

Example 1-5. The `switch` statement

```
putstr("Enter a month number: ");
var monthNum = readline();
var monthName;
switch (monthNum) {
    case "1":
        monthName = "January";
```

```
        break;
    case "2":
        monthName = "February";
        break;
    case "3":
        monthName = "March";
        break;
    case "4":
        monthName = "April";
        break;
    case "5":
        monthName = "May";
        break;
    case "6":
        monthName = "June";
        break;
    case "7":
        monthName = "July";
        break;
    case "8":
        monthName = "August";
        break;
    case "9":
        monthName = "September";
        break;
    case "10":
        monthName = "October";
        break;
    case "11":
        monthName = "November";
        break;
    case "12":
        monthName = "December";
        break;
    default:
        print("Bad input");
}
print(monthName);
```

Is this the most efficient way to solve this problem? No, but it does a great job of demonstrating how the switch statement works.

One major difference between the JavaScript switch statement and switch statements in other programming languages is that the expression that is being tested in the statement can be of any data type, as opposed to an integral data type, as required by languages such as C++ and Java. In fact, you'll notice in the previous example that we use the month numbers as strings, rather than converting them to numbers, since we can compare strings using the switch statement in JavaScript.

Repetition Constructs

Many of the algorithms we study in this book are repetitive in nature. We use two repetition constructs in this book—the `while` loop and the `for` loop.

When we want to execute a set of statements while a condition is true, we use a `while` loop. Example 1-6 demonstrates how the `while` loop works.

Example 1-6. The while loop

```
var number = 1;
var sum = 0;
while (number < 11) {
    sum += number;
    ++number;
}
print(sum); // displays 55
```

When we want to execute a set of statements a specified number of times, we use a `for` loop. Example 1-7 uses a `for` loop to sum the integers 1 through 10.

Example 1-7. Summing integers using a for loop

```
var number = 1;
var sum = 0;
for (var number = 1; number < 11; number++) {
    sum += number;
}
print(sum); // displays 55
```

`for` loops are also used frequently to access the elements of an array, as shown in Example 1-8.

Example 1-8. Using a for loop with an array

```
var numbers = [3, 7, 12, 22, 100];
var sum = 0;
for (var i = 0; i < numbers.length; ++i) {
    sum += numbers[i];
}
print(sum); // displays 144
```

Functions

JavaScript provides the means to define both value-returning functions and functions that don't return values (sometimes called *subprocedures* or *void functions*).

Example 1-9 demonstrates how value-returning functions are defined and called in JavaScript.

Example 1-9. A value-returning function

```
function factorial(number) {
   var product = 1;
   for (var i = number; i >= 1; --i) {
      product *= i;
   }
   return product;
}

print(factorial(4)); // displays 24
print(factorial(5)); // displays 120
print(factorial(10)); // displays 3628800
```

Example 1-10 illustrates how to write a function that is used not for its return value, but for the operations it performs.

Example 1-10. A subprocedure or void function in JavaScript

```
function curve(arr, amount) {
   for (var i = 0; i < arr.length; ++i) {
      arr[i] += amount;
   }
}

var grades = [77, 73, 74, 81, 90];
curve(grades, 5);
print(grades); // displays 82,78,79,86,95
```

All function parameters in JavaScript are passed by value, and there are no reference parameters. However, there are reference objects, such as arrays, which are passed to functions by reference, as was demonstrated in Example 1-10.

Variable Scope

The *scope* of a variable refers to where in a program a variable's value can be accessed. The scope of a variable in JavaScript is defined as *function scope*. This means that a variable's value is visible within the function definition where the variable is declared and defined and within any functions that are nested within that function.

Newer versions of ECMAScript do provide the capability of scoping variables at the block level, using the `let` statement. However, the support for `let` is still limited, and not critical to the core purpose of the book, so we'll stick with widely supported, basic JavaScript functionality.

When a variable is defined outside of a function, in the main program, the variable is said to have *global* scope, which means its value can be accessed by any part of a program, including functions. The following short program demonstrates how global scope works:

```
function showScope() {
    return scope;
}

var scope = "global";
print(scope); // displays "global"
print(showScope()); // displays "global"
```

The function `showScope()` can access the variable `scope` because `scope` is a global variable. Global variables can be declared at any place in a program, either before or after function definitions.

Now watch what happens when we define a second `scope` variable within the `showScope()` function:

```
function showScope() {
    var scope = "local";
    return scope;
}

var scope = "global";
print(scope); // displays "global"
print(showScope()); // displays "local"
```

The `scope` variable defined in the `showScope()` function has local scope, while the `scope` variable defined in the main program is a global variable. Even though the two variables have the same name, their scopes are different, and their values are different when accessed within the area of the program where they are defined.

All of this behavior is normal and expected. However, it can all change if you leave off the keyword `var` in the variable definitions. JavaScript allows you to define variables without using the `var` keyword, but when you do, that variable automatically has global scope, even if defined within a function.

Example 1-11 demonstrates the ramifications of leaving off the `var` keyword when defining variables.

Example 1-11. The ramification of overusing global variables

```
function showScope() {
    scope = "local";
    return scope;
}

scope = "global";
print(scope); // displays "global"
print(showScope()); // displays "local"
print(scope); // displays "local"
```

In Example 1-11, because the scope variable inside the function is not declared with the var keyword, when the string "local" is assigned to the variable, we are actually changing the value of the scope variable in the main program. You should always begin every definition of a variable with the var keyword to keep things like this from happening.

Earlier, we mentioned that JavaScript has function scope. This means that JavaScript does not have *block* scope, unlike many other modern programming languages. With block scope, you can declare a variable within a block of code and the variable is not accessible outside of that block, as you typically see with a C++ or Java for loop:

```
for (int i = 1; i <=10; ++i) {
    cout << "Hello, world!" << endl;
}
```

Even though JavaScript does not have block scope, we pretend like it does when we write for loops in this book:

```
for (var i = 1; i <= 10; ++i ) {
    print("Hello, world!");
}
```

We don't want to be the cause of you picking up bad programming habits.

Recursion

Function calls can be made recursively in JavaScript. The factorial() function defined earlier can also be written recursively, like this:

```
function factorial(number) {
    if (number == 1) {
        return number;
    }
    else {
        return number * factorial(number-1);
    }
}

print(factorial(5));
```

When a function is called recursively, the results of the function's computation are temporarily suspended while the recursion is in progress. To demonstrate how this works, here is a diagram for the `factorial()` function when the argument passed to the function is 5:

```
5 * factorial(4)
5 * 4 * factorial(3)
5 * 4 * 3 * factorial(2)
5 * 4 * 3 * 2 * factorial(1)
5 * 4 * 3 * 2 * 1
5 * 4 * 3 * 2
5 * 4 * 6
5 * 24
120
```

Several of the algorithms discussed in this book use recursion. For the most part, JavaScript is capable of handling fairly deep recursive calls (this is an example of a relatively shallow recursive call); but in one or two situations, an algorithm requires a deeper recursive call than JavaScript can handle and we instead pursue an iterative solution to the algorithm. You should keep in mind that any function that uses recursion can be rewritten in an iterative manner.

Objects and Object-Oriented Programming

The data structures discussed in this book are implemented as objects. JavaScript provides many different ways for creating and using objects. In this section we demonstrate the techniques used in this book for creating objects and for creating and using an object's functions and properties.

Objects are created by defining a constructor function that includes declarations for an object's properties and functions, followed by definitions for the functions. Here is the constructor function for a checking account object:

```
function Checking(amount) {
    this.balance = amount; // property
    this.deposit = deposit; // function
    this.withdraw = withdraw; // function
    this.toString = toString; // function
}
```

The `this` keyword is used to tie each function and property to an object instance. Now let's look at the function definitions for the preceding declarations:

```
function deposit(amount) {
    this.balance += amount;
}

function withdraw(amount) {
    if (amount <= this.balance) {
        this.balance -= amount;
```

```
        }
        if (amount > this.balance) {
            print("Insufficient funds");
        }
    }

    function toString() {
        return "Balance: " + this.balance;
    }
```

Again, we have to use the this keyword with the balance property in order for the interpreter to know which object's balance property we are referencing.

Example 1-12 provides the complete definition for the checking object along with a test program.

Example 1-12. Defining and using the Checking object

```
function Checking(amount) {
    this.balance = amount;
    this.deposit = deposit;
    this.withdraw = withdraw;
    this.toString = toString;
}

function deposit(amount) {
    this.balance += amount;
}

function withdraw(amount) {
    if (amount <= this.balance) {
        this.balance -= amount;
    }
    if (amount > this.balance) {
        print("Insufficient funds");
    }
}

function toString() {
    return "Balance: " + this.balance;
}

var account = new Checking(500);
account.deposit(1000);
print(account.toString()); // Balance: 1500
account.withdraw(750);
print(account.toString()); // Balance: 750
account.withdraw(800); // displays "Insufficient funds"
print(account.toString()); // Balance: 750
```

Summary

This chapter provided an overview of the way we use JavaScript throughout the rest of the book. We try to follow a programming style that is common to many programmers who are accustomed to using C-style languages such as C++ and Java. Of course, JavaScript has many conventions that do not follow the rules of those languages, and we certainly point those out (such as the declaration and use of variables) and show you the correct way to use the language. We also follow as many of the good JavaScript programming practices outlined by authors such as John Resig, Douglas Crockford, and others as we can. As responsible programmers, we need to keep in mind that it is just as important that our programs be readable by humans as it is that they be correctly executed by computers.

CHAPTER 2

Arrays

The array is the most common data structure in computer programming. Every programming language includes some form of array. Because arrays are built-in, they are usually very efficient and are considered good choices for many data storage purposes. In this chapter we explore how arrays work in JavaScript and when to use them.

JavaScript Arrays Defined

The standard definition for an array is a linear collection of elements, where the elements can be accessed via indices, which are usually integers used to compute offsets. Most computer programming languages have these types of arrays. JavaScript, on the other hand, has a different type of array altogether.

A JavaScript array is actually a specialized type of JavaScript object, with the indices being property names that can be integers used to represent offsets. The specification states that array indices are converted to a string before storage, but most JavaScript engines perform optimizations under the hood to make the operation more efficient.

 One of the better descriptions of JavaScript Arrays and how they work is "Arrays in JavaScript" (*http://www.2ality.com/2012/12/ arrays.html*) by Dr. Axel Rauschmayer.

While JavaScript arrays are, strictly speaking, JavaScript objects, they are specialized objects categorized internally as arrays. The Array is one of the recognized JavaScript object types, and as such, there is a set of properties and functions you can use with arrays.

Using Arrays

Arrays in JavaScript are very flexible. There are several different ways to create arrays, access array elements, and perform tasks such as searching and sorting the elements stored in an array. More recent versions of JavaScript (JavaScript 1.5 and up) also includes array functions that allow programmers to work with arrays using functional programming techniques. We demonstrate many of these techniques in the following sections.

Creating Arrays

The simplest way to create an array is by declaring an array variable using an Array literal [ ]:

```
var numbers = [];
```

When you create an array in this manner, you have an array with length of 0. You can verify this by calling the built-in length property:

```
print(numbers.length); // displays 0
```

Another way to create an array is to declare an array variable with a set of elements inside the [ ] operator:

```
var numbers = [1,2,3,4,5];
print(numbers.length); // displays 5
```

You can also create an array by calling the Array constructor:

```
var numbers = new Array();
print(numbers.length); // displays 0
```

You can call the Array constructor with a set of elements as arguments to the constructor:

```
var numbers = new Array(1,2,3,4,5);
print(numbers.length); // displays 5
```

Finally, you can create an array by calling the Array constructor with a single argument specifying the length of the array:

```
var numbers = new Array(10);
print(numbers.length); // displays 10
```

Unlike many other programming languages, but common for most scripting languages, JavaScript array elements do not all have to be of the same type:

```
var objects = [1, "Joe", true, null];
```

We can verify that an object is an array by calling the Array.isArray() function, like this:

```
var numbers = 3;
var arr = [7,4,1776];
print(Array.isArray(numbers)); // displays false
print(Array.isArray(arr)); // displays true
```

We've covered several techniques for creating arrays. As for which function is best, most JavaScript experts recommend using the [ ] operator, saying it is more efficient than calling the Array constructor (see *JavaScript: The Definitive Guide* [O'Reilly] and *JavaScript: The Good Parts* [O'Reilly]).

Accessing and Writing Array Elements

Data is assigned to array elements using the [ ] operator in an assignment statement. For example, the following loop assigns the values 1 through 100 to an array:

```
var nums = [];
for (var i = 0; i < 100; ++i) {
    nums[i] = i+1;
}
```

Array elements are also accessed using the [ ] operator. For example:

```
var numbers = [1,2,3,4,5];
var sum = numbers[0] + numbers[1] + numbers[2] + numbers[3] +
        numbers[4];
print(sum); // displays 15
```

Of course, accessing all the elements of an array sequentially is much easier using a for loop:

```
var numbers = [1,2,3,5,8,13,21];
var sum = 0;
for (var i = 0; i < numbers.length; ++i) {
    sum += numbers[i];
}
print(sum); // displays 53
```

Notice that the for loop is controlled using the length property rather than an integer literal. Because JavaScript arrays are objects, they can grow beyond the size specified when they were created. By using the length property, which returns the number of elements currently in the array, you can guarantee that your loop processes all array elements.

Creating Arrays from Strings

Arrays can be created as the result of calling the split() function on a string. This function breaks up a string at a common delimiter, such as a space for each word, and creates an array consisting of the individual parts of the string.

The following short program demonstrates how the `split()` function works on a simple string:

```
var sentence = "the quick brown fox jumped over the lazy dog";
var words = sentence.split(" ");
for (var i = 0; i < words.length; ++i) {
   print("word " + i + ": " + words[i]);
}
```

The output from this program is:

```
word 0: the
word 1: quick
word 2: brown
word 3: fox
word 4: jumped
word 5: over
word 6: the
word 7: lazy
word 8: dog
```

Aggregate Array Operations

There are several aggregate operations you can perform on arrays. First, you can assign one array to another array:

```
var nums = [];
for (var i = 0; i < 10; ++i) {
   nums[i] = i+1;
}
var samenums = nums;
```

However, when you assign one array to another array, you are assigning a reference to the assigned array. When you make a change to the original array, that change is reflected in the other array as well. The following code fragment demonstrates how this works:

```
var nums = [];
for (var i = 0; i < 100; ++i) {
   nums[i] = i+1;
}
var samenums = nums;
nums[0] = 400;
print(samenums[0]); // displays 400
```

This is called a *shallow copy*. The new array simply points to the original array's elements. A better alternative is to make a *deep copy*, so that each of the original array's elements is actually copied to the new array's elements. An effective way to do this is to create a function to perform the task:

```
function copy(arr1, arr2) {
   for (var i = 0; i < arr1.length; ++i) {
```

```
        arr2[i] = arr1[i];
    }
}
```

Now the following code fragment produces the expected result:

```
var nums = [];
for (var i = 0; i < 100; ++i) {
    nums[i] = i+1;
}
var samenums = [];
copy(nums, samenums);
nums[0] = 400;
print(samenums[0]); // displays 1
```

Note, though, that this type of copy works if the Array values are scalar, not objects or arrays, themselves. In the following code, one array's elements are copied to another, but the first two elements are also arrays. The third is a scalar value. The last element of the second array element in the original array is changed, as is the scalar value. The second array is then printed out to the `console()` (rather than `print()`) in order to display the actual structure.

```
var test = [[1,2,3],[4,5,8],10];
var test2 = [];

for (var i = 0; i < test.length; i++) {
    test2[i] = test[i];
}

test[1][2] = 6;
test[2] = 20;
console.log(test2);
```

The result is:

```
[[1, 2, 3], [4, 5, 6], 10]
```

The array element change is reflected in the copy, but not the scalar value change.

I used `console()` because of the nature of the JavaScript Shell program. Another aggregate operation you can perform with arrays is displaying the contents of an array using a function such as `print()`. For example:

```
var nums = [1,2,3,4,5];
print(nums);
```

will produce the following output:

```
1,2,3,4,5
```

This output may not be particularly useful, but you can use it to display the contents of an array when all you need is a simple list.

Accessor Functions

JavaScript provides a set of functions you can use to access the elements of an array. These functions, called *accessor* functions, return some representation of the target array as their return values.

Searching for a Value

One of the most commonly used accessor functions is indexOf(), which looks to see if the argument passed to the function is found in the array. If the argument is contained in the array, the function returns the index position of the argument. If the argument is not found in the array, the function returns -1. Here is an example:

```
var names = ["David", "Cynthia", "Raymond", "Clayton", "Jennifer"];
putstr("Enter a name to search for: ");
var name = readline();
var position = names.indexOf(name);
if (position >= 0) {
   print("Found " + name + " at position " + position);
}
else {
   print(name + " not found in array.");
}
```

If you run this program and enter **Cynthia**, the program will output:

```
Found Cynthia at position 1
```

If you enter **Joe**, the output is:

```
Joe not found in array.
```

If you have multiple occurrences of the same data in an array, the indexOf() function will always return the position of the first occurrence. A similar function, lastIndexOf(), will return the position of the last occurrence of the argument in the array, or -1 if the argument isn't found. Here is an example:

```
var names = ["David", "Mike", "Cynthia", "Raymond", "Clayton", "Mike",
             "Jennifer"];
var name = "Mike";
var firstPos = names.indexOf(name);
print("First found " + name + " at position " + firstPos);
var lastPos = names.lastIndexOf(name);
print("Last found " + name + " at position " + lastPos);
```

The output from this program is:

```
First found Mike at position 1
Last found Mike at position 5
```

String Representations of Arrays

There are two functions that return string representations of an array: join() and toString(). Both functions return a string containing the elements of the array delimited by commas. Here are some examples:

```
var names = ["David", "Cynthia", "Raymond", "Clayton", "Mike", "Jennifer"];
var namestr = names.join();
print(namestr);  // David,Cynthia,Raymond,Clayton,Mike,Jennifer
namestr = names.toString();
print(namestr); // David,Cynthia,Raymond,Clayton,Mike,Jennifer
```

When you call the print() function with an array name, it automatically calls the toString() function for that array:

```
print(names); // David,Cynthia,Raymond,Clayton,Mike,Jennifer
```

Creating New Arrays from Existing Arrays

There are two accessor functions that allow you create new arrays from existing arrays: concat() and splice(). The concat() function allows you to put together two or more arrays to create a new array, and the splice() function allows you to create a new array from a subset of an existing array.

Let's look first at how concat() works. The function is called from an existing array, and its argument is another existing array. The argument is concatenated to the end of the array calling concat(). The following program demonstrates how concat() works:

```
var cisDept = ["Mike", "Clayton", "Terrill", "Danny", "Jennifer"];
var dmpDept = ["Raymond", "Cynthia", "Bryan"];
var itDiv = cisDept.concat(dmpDept);
print(itDiv);
itDiv = dmpDept.concat(cisDept);
print(itDiv);
```

The program outputs:

```
Mike,Clayton,Terrill,Danny,Jennifer,Raymond,Cynthia,Bryan
Raymond,Cynthia,Bryan,Mike,Clayton,Terrill,Danny,Jennifer
```

The first output line shows the data from the cis array first, and the second output line shows the data from the dmp array first.

The splice() function creates a new array by adding new contents while removing existing. The arguments to the function are the starting position for taking the splice and the number of elements to take from the existing array. Here is how the method works:

```
var itDiv = ["Mike","Clayton","Terrill","Raymond","Cynthia","Danny","Jennifer"];
var dmpDept = itDiv.splice(3,3);
```

```
var cisDept = itDiv;
print(dmpDept); // Raymond,Cynthia,Danny
print(cisDept); // Mike,Clayton,Terrill,Jennifer
```

See the Mozilla Developer Network website (*http://mzl.la/1gmmlQ5*) for more information.

Mutator Functions

JavaScript has a set of *mutator* functions that allow you to modify the contents of an array without referencing the individual elements. These functions often make hard techniques easy, as you'll see below.

Adding Elements to an Array

There are two mutator functions for adding elements to an array: push() and unshift(). The push() function adds an element to the end of an array:

```
var nums = [1,2,3,4,5];
print(nums); // 1,2,3,4,5
nums.push(6);
print(nums); // 1,2,3,4,5,6
```

Using push() is more intuitive than using the length property to extend an array:

```
var nums = [1,2,3,4,5];
print(nums); // 1,2,3,4,5
nums[nums.length] = 6;
print(nums); // 1,2,3,4,5,6
```

Adding data to the beginning of an array is much harder than adding data to the end of an array. To do so without the benefit of a mutator function, each existing element of the array has to be shifted up one position before the new data is added. Here is some code to illustrate this scenario:

```
var nums = [2,3,4,5];
var newnum = 1;
var N = nums.length;
for (var i = N; i >= 0; --i) {
    nums[i] = nums[i-1];
}
nums[0] = newnum;
print(nums); // 1,2,3,4,5
```

This code becomes more inefficient as the number of elements stored in the array increases.

The mutator function for adding array elements to the beginning of an array is unshift(). Here is how the function works:

```
var nums = [2,3,4,5];
print(nums); // 2,3,4,5
var newnum = 1;
nums.unshift(newnum);
print(nums); // 1,2,3,4,5
nums = [3,4,5];
nums.unshift(newnum,2);
print(nums); // 1,2,3,4,5
```

The second call to unshift() demonstrates that you can add multiple elements to an array with one call to the function.

Removing Elements from an Array

Removing an element from the end of an array is easy using the pop() mutator function:

```
var nums = [1,2,3,4,5,9];
nums.pop();
print(nums); // 1,2,3,4,5
```

Without mutator functions, removing elements from the beginning of an array requires shifting elements toward the beginning of the array, causing the same inefficiency we see when adding elements to the beginning of an array:

```
var nums = [9,1,2,3,4,5];
print(nums);
for (var i = 0; i < nums.length; ++i) {
    nums[i] = nums[i+1];
}
print(nums); // 1,2,3,4,5,
```

Besides the fact that we have to shift the elements down to collapse the array, we are also left with an extra element. We know this because of the extra comma we see when we display the array contents.If we used console.log() we'd see that the last element is now undefined.

The mutator function we need to remove an element from the beginning of an array is shift(). Here is how the function works:

```
var nums = [9,1,2,3,4,5];
nums.shift();
print(nums); // 1,2,3,4,5
```

You'll notice there are no extra elements left at the end of the array. Both pop() and shift() return the values they remove, so you can collect the values in a variable:

```
var nums = [6,1,2,3,4,5];
var first = nums.shift(); // first gets the value 9
nums.push(first);
print(nums); // 1,2,3,4,5,6
```

Adding and Removing Elements from the Middle of an Array

Trying to add or remove elements at the middle of an array leads to the same problems we find when trying to add or remove elements from the beginning of an array —both operations require shifting array elements either toward the beginning or toward the end of the array. However, there is one mutator function we can use to add or remove elements from the middle of an array—splice().

To add elements to an array using splice(), you have to provide the following arguments:

- The starting index (where you want to begin adding elements)
- The number of elements to remove (0 when you are adding elements)
- The elements you want to add to the array

Let's look at a simple example. The following program adds three numbers to the middle of an array of numbers:

```
var nums = [1,2,3,7,8,9];
nums.splice(3,0,4,5,6);
print(nums); // 1,2,3,4,5,6,7,8,9
```

Here is an example of using splice() to remove elements from an array:

```
var nums = [1,2,3,100,200,300,400,4,5];
nums.splice(3,4);
print(nums); // 1,2,3,4,5
```

Putting Array Elements in Order

The last two mutator functions are used to arrange array elements into some type of order. The first of these, reverse(), reverses the order of the elements of an array. Here is an example of its use:

```
var nums = [1,2,3,4,5];
nums.reverse();
print(nums); // 5,4,3,2,1
```

We often need to sort the elements of an array into order. The mutator function for this task, sort(), works very well with strings:

```
var names = ["David","Mike","Cynthia","Clayton","Bryan","Raymond"];
names.sort();
print(names); // Bryan,Clayton,Cynthia,David,Mike,Raymond
```

But sort() does not work so well with numbers:

```
var nums = [3,1,2,100,4,200];
nums.sort();
print(nums); // 1,100,2,200,3,4
```

The `sort()` function sorts data lexicographically, assuming the data elements are strings, even though in the preceding example, the elements are numbers. We can make the `sort()` function work correctly for numbers by passing in an ordering function as the first argument to the function, which `sort()` will then use to sort the array elements. This is the function that `sort()` will use when comparing pairs of array elements to determine their correct order.

For numbers, the ordering function can simply subtract one number from another number. If the number returned is negative, the left operand is less than the right operand; if the number returned is zero, the left operand is equal to the right operand; and if the number returned is positive, the left operand is greater than the right operand.

With this in mind, let's rerun the previous small program using an ordering function:

```
function compare(num1, num2) {
    return num1 - num2;
}

var nums = [3,1,2,100,4,200];
nums.sort(compare);
print(nums); // 1,2,3,4,100,200
```

The `sort()` function uses the `compare()` function to sort the array elements numerically rather than lexicographically.

Iterator Functions

The final set of array functions we examine are *iterator* functions. These functions apply a function to each element of an array, either returning a value, a set of values, or a new array after applying the function to each element of an array.

Non–Array-Generating Iterator Functions

The first group of iterator functions we'll discuss do not generate a new array; instead, they either perform an operation on each element of an array or generate a single value from an array.

The first of these functions is `forEach()`. This function takes a function as an argument and applies the called function to each element of an array. Here is an example of how it works:

```
function square(num) {
    print(num, num * num);
}

var nums = [1,2,3,4,5,6,7,8,9,10];
nums.forEach(square);
```

The output from this program is:

```
1 1
2 4
3 9
4 16
5 25
6 36
7 49
8 64
9 81
10 100
```

The next iterator function, every(), applies a Boolean function to an array and returns true if the function can return true for every element in the array. Here is an example:

```
function isEven(num) {
    return num % 2 == 0;
}

var nums = [2,4,6,8,10];
var even = nums.every(isEven);
if (even) {
    print("all numbers are even");
}
else {
    print("not all numbers are even");
}
```

The program displays:

```
all numbers are even
```

If we change the array to:

```
var nums = [2,4,6,7,8,10];
```

the program displays:

```
not all numbers are even
```

The some() function will take a Boolean function and return true if at least one of the elements in the array meets the criterion of the Boolean function. For example:

```
function isEven(num) {
    return num % 2 == 0;
}

var nums = [1,2,3,4,5,6,7,8,9,10];
var someEven = nums.some(isEven);
if (someEven) {
    print("some numbers are even");
}
else {
```

```
      print("no numbers are even");
    }
    nums = [1,3,5,7,9];
    someEven = nums.some(isEven);
    if (someEven) {
      print("some numbers are even");
    }
    else {
      print("no numbers are even");
    }
```

The output from this program is:

```
some numbers are even
no numbers are even
```

The reduce() function applies a function to an accumulator and the successive elements of an array until the end of the array is reached, yielding a single value. Here is an example of using reduce() to compute the sum of the elements of an array:

```
function add(runningTotal, currentValue) {
    return runningTotal + currentValue;
}

var nums = [1,2,3,4,5,6,7,8,9,10];
var sum = nums.reduce(add);
print(sum); // displays 55
```

The reduce() function, in conjunction with the add() function, works from left to right, computing a running sum of the array elements, like this:

```
add(1,2) -> 3
add(3,3) -> 6
add(6,4) -> 10
add(10,5) -> 15
add(15,6) -> 21
add(21,7) -> 28
add(28,8) -> 36
add(36,9) -> 45
add(45,10) -> 55
```

We can also use reduce() with strings to perform concatenation:

```
function concat(accumulatedString, item) {
    return accumulatedString + item;
}

var words = ["the ", "quick ","brown ", "fox "];
var sentence = words.reduce(concat);
print(sentence); // displays "the quick brown fox"
```

JavaScript also provides a reduceRight() function, which works similarly to reduce(), only working from the righthand side of the array to the left, instead of from left to right. The following program uses `reduceRight()` to reverse the elements of an array:

```
function concat(accumulatedString, item) {
    return accumulatedString + item;
}

var words = ["the ", "quick ","brown ", "fox "];
var sentence = words.reduceRight(concat);
print(sentence); // displays "fox brown quick the"
```

Iterator Functions That Return a New Array

There are two iterator functions that return new arrays: `map()` and `filter()`. The `map()` function works like the `forEach()` function, applying a function to each element of an array. The difference between the two functions is that `map()` returns a new array with the results of the function application. Here is an example:

```
function curve(grade) {
    return grade += 5;
}

var grades = [77, 65, 81, 92, 83];
var newgrades = grades.map(curve);
print(newgrades); // 82, 70, 86, 97, 88
```

Here is an example using strings:

```
function first(word) {
    return word[0];
}

var words = ["for","your","information"];
var acronym = words.map(first);
print(acronym.join("")); // displays "fyi"
```

For this last example, the `acronym` array stores the first letter of each word in the words array. However, if we want to display the elements of the array as a true acronym, we need to get rid of the commas that will be displayed if we just display the array elements using the implied `toString()` function. We accomplish this by calling the `join()` function with the empty string as the separator.

The `filter()` function works similarly to `every()`, but instead of returning `true` if all the elements of an array satisfy a Boolean function, the function returns a new array consisting of those elements that satisfy the Boolean function. Here is an example:

```
function isEven(num) {
    return num % 2 == 0;
}
```

```
function isOdd(num) {
    return num % 2 != 0;
}

var nums = [];
for (var i = 0; i < 20; ++i) {
    nums[i] = i+1;
}
var evens = nums.filter(isEven);
print("Even numbers: ");
print(evens);
var odds = nums.filter(isOdd);
print("Odd numbers: ");
print(odds);
```

This program returns the following output:

```
Even numbers:
2,4,6,8,10,12,14,16,18,20
Odd numbers:
1,3,5,7,9,11,13,15,17,19
```

Here is another interesting use of `filter()`:

```
function passing(num) {
    return num >= 60;
}

var grades = [];
for (var i = 0; i < 20; ++i) {
    grades[i] = Math.floor(Math.random() * 101);
}
var passGrades = grades.filter(passing);
print("All grades: ");
print(grades);
print("Passing grades: ");
print(passGrades);
```

This program displays:

```
All grades:
39,43,89,19,46,54,48,5,13,31,27,95,62,64,35,75,79,88,73,74
Passing grades:
89,95,62,64,75,79,88,73,74
```

Of course, we can also use `filter()` with strings. Here is an example that applies the spelling rule "i before e except after c":

```
function afterc(str) {
    if (str.indexOf("cie") > -1) {
        return true;
    }
    return false;
}
```

```
var words = ["recieve","deceive","percieve","deceit","concieve"];
var misspelled = words.filter(afterc);
print(misspelled); // displays recieve,percieve,concieve
```

Two-Dimensional and Multidimensional Arrays

JavaScript arrays are only one-dimensional, but you can create multidimensional arrays by creating arrays of arrays. In this section we'll describe how to create two-dimensional arrays in JavaScript.

Creating Two-Dimensional Arrays

A two-dimensional array is structured like a spreadsheet with rows and columns. To create a two-dimensional array in JavaScript, we have to create an array and then make each element of the array an array as well. At the very least, we need to know the number of rows we want the array to contain. With that information, we can create a two-dimensional array with *n* rows and one column:

```
var twod = [];
var rows = 5;
for (var i = 0; i < rows; ++i) {
    twod[i] = [];
}
```

The problem with this approach is that each element of the array is set to undefined. A better way to create a two-dimensional array is to follow the example from *Java-Script: The Good Parts* (O'Reilly, p. 64). Crockford extends the JavaScript array object with a function that sets the number of rows and columns and sets each value to a value passed to the function. Here is his definition:

```
Array.matrix = function(numrows, numcols, initial) {
    var arr = [];
    for (var i = 0; i < numrows; ++i) {
        var columns = [];
        for (var j = 0; j < numcols; ++j) {
            columns[j] = initial;
        }
        arr[i] = columns;
    }
    return arr;
};
```

Here is some code to test the definition:

```
var nums = Array.matrix(5,5,0);
print(nums[1][1]); // displays 0
var names = Array.matrix(3,3,"");
names[1][2] = "Joe";
print(names[1][2]); // display "Joe"
```

We can also create a two-dimensional array and initialize it to a set of values in one line:

```
var grades = [[89, 77, 78],[76, 82, 81],[91, 94, 89]];
print(grades[2][2]); // displays 89
```

For small data sets, this is the easiest way to create a two-dimensional array.

Processing Two-Dimensional Array Elements

There are two fundamental patterns used to process the elements of a two-dimensional array. One pattern emphasizes accessing array elements by columns, and the other pattern emphasizes accessing array elements by rows. We will use the grades array created in the preceding code fragment to demonstrate how these patterns work.

For both patterns, we use a set of nested for loops. For columnar processing, the outer loop moves through the rows, and the inner loop processes the columns. For the grades array, think of each row as a set of grades for one student. We can compute the average for each student's grades by adding each grade on the row to a total variable and then dividing total by the total number of grades on that row. Here is the code for that process:

```
var grades = [[89, 77, 78],[76, 82, 81],[91, 94, 89]];
var total = 0;
var average = 0.0;
for (var row = 0; row < grades.length; ++row) {
    for (var col = 0; col < grades[row].length; ++col) {
        total += grades[row][col];
    }
    average = total / grades[row].length;
    print("Student " + parseInt(row+1) + " average: " +
        average.toFixed(2));
    total = 0;
    average = 0.0;
}
```

The inner loop is controlled by the expression:

```
col < grades[row].length
```

This works because each row contains an array, and that array has a length property we can use to determine how many columns there are in the row.

The grade average for each student is rounded to two decimals using the toFixed(n) function.

Here is the output from the program:

```
Student 1 average: 81.33
Student 2 average: 79.67
Student 3 average: 91.33
```

To perform a row-wise computation, we simply have to flip the for loops so that the outer loop controls the columns and the inner loop controls the rows. Here is the calculation for each test:

```
var grades = [[89, 77, 78],[76, 82, 81],[91, 94, 89]];
var total = 0;
var average = 0.0;
for (var col = 0; col < grades.length; ++col) {
   for (var row = 0; row < grades[col].length; ++row) {
      total += grades[row][col];
   }


   average = total / grades[col].length;
   print("Test " + parseInt(col+1) + " average: " +
         average.toFixed(2));
   total = 0;
   average = 0.0;
}
```

The output from this program is:

```
Test 1 average: 85.33
Test 2 average: 84.33
Test 3 average: 82.67
```

Jagged Arrays

A *jagged* array is an array where the rows in the array may have a different number of elements. One row may have three elements, while another row may have five elements, while yet another row may have just one element. Many programming languages have problems handling jagged arrays, but JavaScript does not since we can compute the length of any row.

To give you an example, imagine the grades array where students have an unequal number of grades recorded. We can still compute the correct average for each student without changing the program at all:

```
var grades = [[89, 77],[76, 82, 81],[91, 94, 89, 99]];
var total = 0;
var average = 0.0;
for (var row = 0; row < grades.length; ++row) {
   for (var col = 0; col < grades[row].length; ++col) {
      total += grades[row][col];
   }
   average = total / grades[row].length;
   print("Student " + parseInt(row+1) + " average: " +
         average.toFixed(2));
```

```
        total = 0;
        average = 0.0;
    }
```

Notice that the first student only has two grades, while the second student has three grades, and the third student has four grades. Because the program computes the length of the row in the inner loop, this jaggedness doesn't cause any problems. Here is the output from the program:

```
Student 1 average: 83.00
Student 2 average: 79.67
Student 3 average: 93.25
```

Arrays of Objects

All of the examples in this chapter have consisted of arrays whose elements have been primitive data types, such as numbers and strings. Arrays can also consist of objects, and all the functions and properties of arrays work with objects.

For example:

```
function Point(x,y) {
    this.x = x;
    this.y = y;
}

function displayPts(arr) {
    for (var i = 0; i < arr.length; ++i) {
        print(arr[i].x + ", " + arr[i].y);
    }
}

var p1 = new Point(1,2);
var p2 = new Point(3,5);
var p3 = new Point(2,8);
var p4 = new Point(4,4);
var points = [p1,p2,p3,p4];
for (var i = 0; i < points.length; ++i) {
    print("Point " + parseInt(i+1) + ": " + points[i].x + ", " +
        points[i].y);
}
var p5 = new Point(12,-3);
points.push(p5);
print("After push: ");
displayPts(points);
points.shift();
print("After shift: ");
displayPts(points);
```

The output from this program is:

```
Point 1: 1, 2
Point 2: 3, 5
Point 3: 2, 8
Point 4: 4, 4
After push:
1, 2
3, 5
2, 8
4, 4
12, -3
After shift:
3, 5
2, 8
4, 4
12, -3
```

The point 12, -3 is added to the array using push(), and the point 1, 2 is removed from the array using shift().

Arrays in Objects

We can use arrays to store complex data in an object. Many of the data structures we study in this book are implemented as class objects with an underlying array used to store data.

The following example demonstrates many of the techniques we use throughout the book. In the example, we create an object that stores the weekly observed high temperature. The object has functions for adding a new temperature and computing the average of the temperatures stored in the object. Here is the code:

```
function weekTemps() {
   this.dataStore = [];
   this.add = add;
   this.average = average;
}

function add(temp) {
   this.dataStore.push(temp);
}

function average() {
   var total = 0;
   for (var i = 0; i < this.dataStore.length; ++i) {
      total += this.dataStore[i];
   }
   return total / this.dataStore.length;
}

var thisWeek = new weekTemps();
thisWeek.add(52);
thisWeek.add(55);
```

```
thisWeek.add(61);
thisWeek.add(65);
thisWeek.add(55);
thisWeek.add(50);
thisWeek.add(52);
thisWeek.add(49);
print(thisWeek.average()); // displays 54.875
```

You'll notice the add() function uses the push() function to add elements to the data Store array, using the name add() rather than push(). Using a more intuitive name for an operation is a common technique when defining object functions. Not everyone will understand what it means to push a data element, but everyone knows what it means to add a data element.

Exercises

1. Create a grades object that stores a set of student grades in an object. Provide a function for adding a grade and a function for displaying the student's grade average.

2. Store a set of words in an array and display the contents both forward and backward.

3. Modify the weeklyTemps object in the chapter so that it stores a month's worth of data using a two-dimensional array. Create functions to display the monthly average, a specific week's average, and all the weeks' averages.

4. Create an object that stores individual letters in an array and has a function for displaying the letters as a single word.

CHAPTER 3

Lists

Lists are one of the most common organizing tools people use in their day-to-day lives. We have to-do lists, grocery lists, top-ten lists, bottom-ten lists, and many other types. Our computer programs can also use lists, particularly if we only have a few items to store in list form. Lists are especially useful if we don't have to perform searches on the items in the list or put them into some type of sorted order. When we need to perform long searches or complex sorts, lists become less useful, especially with more complex data structures.

This chapter presents the creation of a simple list class. We start with the definition of a list abstract data type (ADT) and then demonstrate how to implement the ADT. We wrap up the chapter with some problems that are best solved with lists.

A List ADT

In order to design an ADT for a list, we have to provide a definition of the list, including its properties, as well as the operations performed on it and by it.

A list is an ordered sequence of data. Each data item stored in a list is called an *element*. In JavaScript, the elements of a list can be of any data type. There is no predetermined number of elements that can be stored in a list, though the practical limit will be the amount of memory available to the program using the list.

A list with no elements is an *empty* list. The number of elements stored in a list is called the *length* of the list. Internally, the number of elements in a list is kept in a listSize variable. You can *append* an element to the end of a list, or you can *insert* an element into a list after an existing element or at the beginning of a list. Elements are deleted from a list using a *remove* operation. You can also *clear* a list so that all of its current elements are removed.

The elements of a list are displayed using either a `toString()` operation, which displays all the elements, or with a `getElement()` operation, which displays the value of the *current* element.

Lists have properties to describe location. There is the *front* of a list and the *end* of a list. You can move from one element of a list to the next element using the `next()` operation, and you can move backward through a list using the `prev()` operation. You can also move to a numbered position in a list using the `moveTo(n)` operation, where *n* specifies the position to move to. The `currPos` property indicates the current position in a list.

The List ADT does not specify a storage function for a list, but for our implementation will use an array named `dataStore`.

Table 3-1 shows the complete List ADT.

Table 3-1. ADT List

`listSize` (property)	Number of elements in list
`pos` (property)	Current position in list
`length` (property)	Returns the number of elements in list
`clear` (function)	Clears all elements from list
`toString` (function)	Returns string representation of list
`getElement` (function)	Returns element at current position
`insert` (function)	Inserts new element after existing element
`append` (function)	Adds new element to end of list
`remove` (function)	Removes element from list
`front` (function)	Sets current position to first element of list
`end` (function)	Sets current position to last element of list
`previous` (function)	Returns previous element
`next` (function)	Returns next element
`hasPrevious` (function)	Tests if previous element exists

hasNext (function)	Tests if next element exists
currPos (function)	Returns the current position in list
moveTo (function)	Moves the current position to specified position

A List Class Implementation

A List class implementation can be taken straight from the List ADT we just defined. We'll start with a definition of a constructor function, though it is not part of the ADT:

```
function List() {
    this.listSize = 0;
    this.pos = 0;
    this.dataStore = []; // initializes an empty array to store list elements
    this.clear = clear;
    this.find = find;
    this.toString = toString;
    this.insert = insert;
    this.append = append;
    this.remove = remove;
    this.front = front;
    this.end = end;
    this.previous = previous;
    this.next = next;
    this.hasPrevious = hasPrevious;
    this.hasNext = hasNext;
    this.length = length;
    this.currPos = currPos;
    this.moveTo = moveTo;
    this.getElement = getElement;
    this.contains = contains;
}
```

Append: Adding an Element to a List

The first function we'll implement is the append() function. This function appends a new element onto the list at the next available position, which will be equal to the value of the listSize variable:

```
function append(element) {
    this.dataStore[this.listSize++] = element;
}
```

After the element is appended, listSize is incremented by 1.

Remove: Removing an Element from a List

Next, let's see how to remove an element from a list. `remove()` is one of the harder functions to implement in the `List` class. First, we have to find the element in the list, and then we have to remove it and adjust the space in the underlying array to fill the hole left by removing an element. However, we can simplify the process by using the `splice()` mutator function. To start, let's define a helper function, `find()`, for finding the element to remove:

```
function find(element) {
    for (var i = 0; i < this.dataStore.length; ++i) {
        if (this.dataStore[i] == element) {
            return i;
        }
    }
    return -1;
}
```

Find: Finding an Element in a List

The `find` function simply iterates through `dataStore` looking for the specified element. If the element is found, the function returns the position where the element was found. If the element wasn't found, the function returns `-1`, which is a standard value to return when an element can't be found in an array. We can use this value for error checking in the `remove()` function.

The `remove()` function uses the position returned by `find()` to splice the `dataStore` array at that place. After the array is modified, `listSize` is decremented by 1 to reflect the new size of the list. The function returns `true` if an element is removed, and `false` otherwise. Here is the code:

```
function remove(element) {
    var foundAt = this.find(element);
    if (foundAt > -1) {
        this.dataStore.splice(foundAt,1);
        --this.listSize;
        return true;
    }
    return false;
}
```

Length: Determining the Number of Elements in a List

The `length()` function returns the number of elements in a list:

```
function length() {
    return this.listSize;
}
```

toString: Retrieving a List's Elements

Now is a good time to create a function that allows us to view the elements of a list. Here is the code for a simple `toString()` function:

```
function toString() {
    return this.dataStore;
}
```

Strictly speaking, this function returns an array object and not a string, but its utility is in providing a view of the current state of an object, and just returning the array works adequately for this purpose.

Let's take a break from implementing our `List` class to see how well it works so far. You'll need to comment out the List object's properties assigned to functions that haven't been defined yet. Here is a short test program that exercises the functions we've created so far:

Example 3-1 using `toString()` to display a List

Example 3-1. toString() retrieves contents of a List

```
var names = new List();
names.append("Cynthia");
names.append("Raymond");
names.append("Barbara");
print(names.toString());
names.remove("Raymond");
print(names.toString());
```

The output from this program is:

```
Cynthia,Raymond,Barbara
Cynthia,Barbara
```

Insert: Inserting an Element into a List

The next function to discuss is `insert()`. What if, after removing Raymond from the preceding list, we decide we need to put him back where he was to begin with? An insertion function needs to know where to insert an element, so for now we will say that insertion occurs after a specified element already in the list. With this in mind, here is the definition of the `insert()` function:

```
function insert(element, after) {
    var insertPos = this.find(after);
    if (insertPos > -1) {
        this.dataStore.splice(insertPos+1, 0, element);
        ++this.listSize;
        return true;
    }
}
```

```
      return false;
   }
```

`insert()` uses the helper function `find()` to determine the correct insertion position for the new element by finding the element specified in the `after` argument. Once this position is found, we use `splice()` to insert the new element into the list. Then we increment `listSize` by 1 and return `true` to indicate the insertion was successful.

Clear: Removing All Elements from a List

Next, we need a function to clear out the elements of a list and allow new elements to be entered:

```
function clear() {
   delete this.dataStore;
   this.dataStore = [];
   this.listSize = this.pos = 0;
}
```

The `clear()` function uses the `delete` operator to delete the `dataStore` array, and the next line re-creates the empty array. The last line sets the values of `listSize` and `pos` to 0 to indicate the start of a new list.

Contains: Determining if a Given Value Is in a List

The `contains()` function is useful when you want to check a list to see if a particular value is part of the list. Here is the definition:

```
function contains(element) {
   for (var i = 0; i < this.dataStore.length; ++i) {
      if (this.dataStore[i] == element) {
         return true;
      }
   }
   return false;
}
```

Moving To and Retrieving a List Element

The next two functions allow us to move to a specific element index (`moveTo()`) and then retrieve the element wherever the list index is currently residing (`getEle ment()`):

```
function moveTo(position) {
   this.pos = position;
}

function getElement() {
   return this.dataStore[this.pos];
}
```

There's no error checking incorporated into the function, other than the underlying JavaScript error handling based on accessing a nonexisted Array element. If the code sets the position beyond the end of the Array, and then accesses the element at the position, a value of undefined is returned. You can also incorporate more sophisticated error handling, including throwing an error when accessing a list element that doesn't exist.

Iterating Through a List

This final set of functions enable iteration through a list. To enable the functionality, I turned to the Java List implementation, especially its iterator functions next(), previous(), hasNext(), and hasPrevious(), since they can be effectively used with our underlying array structure while still remaining true to the concept of the list.

The hasNext() function tests to see if there's any additional elements to the right of the existing list position. The next() method returns the next element to the right, and then increments the list position counter. The hasPrevious() function tests to see if there's any additional elements to the left of the existing list position. The previous() function then fetches the element to the left, after first decrementing the cursor position. The key understanding to take away from next() and previous() is that the first previous() call after the last call to next() returns the same element.

The final three functions are front() and end(), to move the current position to the front of the list, or the end, and currPos(), returning the current position.

```
function previous() {
   return this.dataStore[--this.pos];
}

function next() {
   return this.dataStore[this.pos++];
}

function hasNext() {
  if (this.pos > this.listSize -1) {
    return false;
  } else {
    return true;
  }
}

function hasPrevious() {
  if (this.pos <= 0) {
    return false;
  } else {
    return true;
  }
}
```

```
function front() {
  this.pos = 0;
}

function end() {
  this.pos = this.listSize - 1;
}

function currPos() {
  return pos;
}
```

Example 3-2 creates a new list of names to demonstrate how these functions work.

Example 3-2. Test various List functions

```
var names = new List();
names.append("Clayton");
names.append("Raymond");
names.append("Cynthia");
names.append("Jennifer");
names.append("Bryan");
names.append("Danny");
```

Now let's move to the first element of the list and display it:

```
names.front();
print(names.getElement()); // displays Clayton
```

Calling `next()` and printing the name displays the same name, since `next()` increments the `List` index only after returning the element:

```
print(names.next());  // displays Clayton
```

Now we'll move forward twice and backward twice, displaying the current element to demonstrate how the `previous()` function works:

```
print(names.next()); // displays Raymond
names.next();
names.previous();
print(names.previous()); // displays Raymond
```

The behavior we've demonstrated in these past few code fragments is captured in the concept of an *iterator*. We explore iterators in the next section.

Iterating Through a List

An iterator allows us to traverse a list without referencing the internal storage mechanism of the `List` class. The functions `front()`, `end()`, `previous()`, `nextious()`, has

Next(), and hasPrevious() provide an implementation of an iterator for our List class. Some advantages to using iterators over using array indexing include:

- Not having to worry about the underlying data storage structure when accessing list elements
- Being able to update the list and not having to update the iterator, where an index becomes invalid when a new element is added to the list
- Providing a uniform means of accessing elements for different types of data stores used in the implemenation of a List class

With these advantages in mind, here is how to use an iterator to traverse through a list:

```
for (names.front(); names.hasNext();) {
  print(names.next());
}
```

The for loop starts by setting the current position to the front of the list. The loop continues until hasNext() returns false. No incrementer is necessary in the for loop, as next() increments the List position.

We can also traverse a list backward using an iterator. Here is the code:

```
for (names.end(); names.hasPrevious();) {
  console.log(names.previous());
}
```

The loop starts at the last element of the list and moves backward using the previous() function while hasPrevious() returns true.

Iterators are used only to move through a list and should not be combined with any functions for adding or removing items from a list.

A List-Based Application

To demonstrate how to use lists, we are going to build a system that can be used in the simulation of a video-rental kiosk system such as Redbox.

Reading Text Files

In order to get the list of videos available in the kiosk into our program, we need to be able to read the data from a file. We first have to create a text file that contains the list of videos available using a text editor. We name the file films.txt. Here are the contents of the files (these movies are the top 20 movies as voted on by IMDB users as of October 5, 2013):

1. *The Shawshank Redemption*

2. *The Godfather*

3. *The Godfather: Part II*

4. *Pulp Fiction*

5. *The Good, the Bad and the Ugly*

6. *12 Angry Men*

7. *Schindler's List*

8. *The Dark Knight*

9. *The Lord of the Rings: The Return of the King*

10. *Fight Club*

11. *Star Wars: Episode V - The Empire Strikes Back*

12. *One Flew Over the Cuckoo's Nest*

13. *The Lord of the Rings: The Fellowship of the Ring*

14. *Inception*

15. *Goodfellas*

16. *Star Wars*

17. *Seven Samurai*

18. *The Matrix*

19. *Forrest Gump*

20. *City of God*

Now we need a code fragment to read the contents of the file into our program:

```
var movies = read('films.txt').split("\n");+\
```

This line performs two tasks. First, it reads the contents of our movies text file into the program, read(*films.txt*); and second, it splits the file into individual lines by using the newline character as a delimiter. This output is then stored as an array in the movies variable.

This line of code works up to a point, but it's not perfect. When the elements of the text file are split into the array, the newline character is replaced with a space. While a single space seems innocuous enough, having an extra space in a string can cause havoc when you are doing string comparisons. So we need to add a loop that strips the space from each array element using the trim() function. This code will work better in a function, so let's create a function to read data from a file and store it in an array:

```
function createArr(file) {
    var arr = read(file).split("\n");
```

```
    for (var i = 0; i < arr.length; ++i) {
        arr[i] = arr[i].trim();
    }
    return arr;
}
```

Using Lists to Manage a Kiosk

The next step is to take the movies array and store its contents in a list. Here is how we do it:

```
var movieList = new List();
for (var i = 0; i < movies.length; ++i) {
    movieList.append(movies[i]);
}
```

Now we can write a function to display the movie list available at the kiosk:

```
function displayList(list) {
    for (list.front(); list.hasNext(); ) {
        print(list.next());
    }
}
```

The displayList() function works fine with native types, such as lists made up of strings, but it won't work for Customer objects, which are defined below. Let's modify the function so that if it discovers that the list is made up of Customer objects, it will display those objects accordingly. Here's the new definition of displayList():

```
function displayList(list) {
    for (list.front(); list.hasNext(); ) {
        var listItem = list.next();
        if (listItem instanceof Customer) {
            print(listItem.name + ", " +
                    listItem.movie);
        }
        else {
            print(listItem);
        }
    }
}
```

We assign the next list item to an internal variable for further manipulation. Remember that next() increments in place, so must only be called once. For each object in the list, we use the instanceof operator to test whether the object is a Customer object. If so, we retrieve the name and the movie the customer has checked out using each of the two properties as an index for retrieving the associated value. If the object is not a Customer, the code simply prints the element.

Now that we have our movie list taken care of, we need to create a list to store the customers who check out movies at the kiosk:

```
var customers = new List();
```

This will contain `Customer` objects, which are made up of the customer's name and the movie checked out. Here is the constructor function for the `Customer` object:

```
function Customer(name, movie) {
    this.name = name;
    this.movie = movie;
}
```

Next, we need a function that allows a customer to check out a movie. This function takes two arguments: the customer's name and the movie he wants to check out. If the movie is available, the function removes the movie from the kiosk's list of movies and adds it to the customer's list. We'll use the `List` class function `contains()` for this task.

Here is the definition for a function to check out a movie:

```
function checkOut(name, movie, movieList, customerList) {
    if (movieList.contains(movie)) {
        var c = new Customer(name, movie);
        customerList.append(c);
        movieList.remove(movie);
    }
    else {
        print(movie + " is not available.");
    }
}
```

The function first checks to see if the movie requested is available. If the movie is available, a `Customer` object is created with the movie's title and the customer's name. The `Customer` object is appended to the customer list, and the movie is removed from the movie list. If the movie is not available, a simple message is displayed indicating such.

We can test the `checkOut()` function with a short program (shown in Example 3-3).

Example 3-3. Test the checkOut() function

```
var movies = createArr("films.txt");
var movieList = new List();
var customers = new List();
for (var i = 0; i < movies.length; ++i) {
    movieList.append(movies[i]);
}
print("Available movies: \n");
displayList(movieList);
checkOut("Jane Doe", "The Godfather", movieList, customers);
print("\nCustomer Rentals: \n");
displayList(customers);
```

The output of the program displays the movie list with `"The Godfather"` removed, followed by the list of customers with movies checked out.

Add some titles to our program's output to make it easier to read, along with some interactive input (see Example 3-4).

Example 3-4. A more user-friendly version of the kiosk program

```
var movies = createArr("films.txt");
var movieList = new List();
var customers = new List();
for (var i = 0; i < movies.length; ++i) {
    movieList.append(movies[i]);
}
print("Available movies: \n");
displayList(movieList);
putstr("\nEnter your name: ");
var name = readline();
putstr("What movie would you like? ");
var movie = readline();
checkOut(name, movie, movieList, customers);
print("\nCustomer Rentals: \n");
displayList(customers);
print("\nMovies Now Available\n");
displayList(movieList);
```

Here is the result of running this program:

```
Available movies:

The Shawshank Redemption
The Godfather
The Godfather: Part II
Pulp Fiction
The Good, the Bad and the Ugly
12 Angry Men
Schindler's List
The Dark Knight
The Lord of the Rings: The Return of the King
Fight Club
Star Wars: Episode V - The Empire Strikes Back
One Flew Over the Cuckoo's Nest
The Lord of the Rings: The Fellowship of the Ring
Inception
Goodfellas
Star Wars
Seven Samurai
The Matrix
Forrest Gump
City of God
```

```
Enter your name: Jane Doe
What movie would you like? The Godfather

Customer Rentals:

Jane Doe, The Godfather

Movies Now Available

The Shawshank Redemption
The Godfather: Part II
Pulp Fiction
The Good, the Bad and the Ugly
12 Angry Men
Schindler's List
The Dark Knight
The Lord of the Rings: The Return of the King
Fight Club
Star Wars: Episode V - The Empire Strikes Back
One Flew Over the Cuckoo's Nest
The Lord of the Rings: The Fellowship of the Ring
Inception
Goodfellas
Star Wars
Seven Samurai
The Matrix
Forrest Gump
City of God
```

We can add other functionality to make our video-rental kiosk system more robust. You will get to explore some of this added functionality in the exercises that follow.

Exercises

1. Write a function that inserts an element into a list only if the element to be inserted is larger than any of the elements currently in the list. Larger can mean either greater than when working with numeric values, or further down in the alphabet, when working with textual values.

2. Write a function that inserts an element into a list only if the element to be inserted is smaller than any of the elements currently in the list.

3. Create a Person class that stores a person's name and their gender. Create a list of at least 10 Person objects. Write a function that displays all the people in the list of the same gender.

4. Modify the video-rental kiosk program so that when a movie is checked out it is added to a list of rented movies. Display this list whenever a customer checks out a movie.

5. Create a check-in function for the video-rental kiosk program so that a returned movies is deleted from the rented movies list and is added back to the available movies list.

CHAPTER 4

Stacks

Lists are a natural form of organization for data. We have already seen how to use the List class to organize data into a list. When the order of the data being stored doesn't matter, or when you don't have to search the data stored, lists work wonderfully. For other applications, however, plain lists are too simple and we need a more complex, list-like data structure.

A list-like structure that can be used to solve many problems in computing is the stack. Stacks are efficient data structures because data can be added or removed only from the top of a stack, making these procedures fast and easy to implement. Stacks are used extensively in programming language implementations for everything from expression evaluation to handling function calls.

Stack Operations

A stack is a list of elements that are accessible only from one end of the list, which is called the top. One common, real-world example of a stack is the stack of trays at a cafeteria. Trays are always removed from the top, and when trays are put back on the stack after being washed, they are placed on the top of the stack. The stack is known as a last-in, first-out (LIFO) data structure.

Because of the last-in, first-out nature of the stack, any element that is not currently at the top of the stack cannot be accessed. To get to an element at the bottom of the stack, you have to dispose of all the elements above it first.

The two primary operations of a stack are adding elements to a stack and taking elements off a stack. Elements are added to a stack using the push operation. Elements are taken off a stack using the pop operation. These operations are illustrated in Figure 4-1.

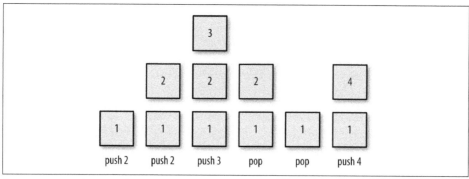

Figure 4-1. Pushing and popping elements of a stack

Another common operation on a stack is viewing the element at the top of a stack. The pop operation visits the top element of a stack, but it permanently removes the element from a stack. The peek operation returns the value stored at the top of a stack without removing it from the stack.

To keep track of where the top element is, as well as keeping track of where to add a new element, we use a top variable that is incremented when we push new elements onto the stack and is decremented when we pop elements off the stack.

While pushing, popping, and peeking are the primary operations associated with a stack, there are other operations we need to perform and properties we need to examine. The clear operation removes all the elements from a stack. The length property holds the number of elements contained in a stack. We also define an empty property to let us know if a stack has no elements in it, though we can use the length property for this as well.

A Stack Implementation

To build a stack, we first need to decide on the underlying data structure we will use to store the stack elements. We will use an array in our implementation.

We begin our stack implementation by defining the constructor function for a Stack class:

```
function Stack() {
    this.dataStore = [];
    this.top = 0;
    this.push = push;
    this.pop = pop;
    this.peek = peek;
}
```

The array that stores the stack elements is named dataStore. The constructor sets it to an empty array. The top variable keeps track of the top of the stack and is initially set to 0 by the constructor, indicating that the 0 position of the array is the top of the stack, at least until an element is pushed onto the stack.

The first function to implement is the push() function. When we push a new element onto a stack, we have to store it in the top position and increment the top variable so that the new top is the next empty position in the array. Here is the code:

```
function push(element) {
    this.dataStore[this.top++] = element;
}
```

Pay particular attention to the placement of the increment operator *after* the call to this.top. Placing the operator there ensures that the current value of top is used to place the new element at the top of the stack before top is incremented.

The pop() function does the reverse of the push() function—it returns the element in the top position of the stack and then decrements the top variable:

```
function pop() {
    return this.dataStore[--this.top];
}
```

The peek() function returns the top element of the stack by accessing the element at the top-1 position of the array:

```
function peek() {
        return this.dataStore[this.top-1];
}
```

If you call the peek() function on an empty stack, you get undefined as the result. That's because there is no value stored at the top position of the stack since it is empty.

There will be situations when you need to know how many elements are stored in a stack. The length() function returns this value by returning the value of top:

```
function length() {
        return this.top;
}
```

Finally, we can clear a stack by simply setting the top variable back to 0, and setting the dataStore array's length to zero:

```
function clear() {
        this.top = 0;
    this.dataStore.length = 0;
}
```

Example 4-1 shows the complete implementation of the Stack class.

Example 4-1. The Stack class

```
load("Stack.js");

function Stack() {
   this.dataStore = [];
   this.top = 0;
   this.push = push;
   this.pop = pop;
   this.peek = peek;
   this.clear = clear;
   this.length = length;
}

function push(element) {
   this.dataStore[this.top++] = element;
}

function peek() {
   return this.dataStore[this.top-1];
}

function pop() {
   return this.dataStore[--this.top];
}

function clear() {
   this.top = 0;
   this.dataStore.length = 0;
}

function length() {
   return this.top;
}
```

Example 4-2 demonstrates a program that tests this implementation.

Example 4-2. Testing the Stack class implementation

```
load("Stack.js");

var s = new Stack();
s.push("David");
s.push("Raymond");
s.push("Bryan");
print("length: " + s.length());
print(s.peek());
var popped = s.pop();
print("The popped element is: " + popped);
print(s.peek());
s.push("Cynthia");
```

```
print(s.peek());
s.clear();
print("length: " + s.length());
print(s.peek());
s.push("Clayton");
print(s.peek());
```

The output from Example 4-2 is:

```
length: 3
Bryan
The popped element is: Bryan
Raymond
Cynthia
length: 0
undefined
Clayton
```

The next-to-last value, undefined, is returned because once a stack is cleared, there is no value in the top position and when we peek at the top of the stack, undefined is returned.

Using the Stack Class

There are several problems for which a stack is the perfect data structure needed for the solution. In this section, we look at several such problems.

Multiple Base Conversions

A stack can be used to convert a number from one base to another base. Given a number, *n*, which we want to convert to a base, *b*, here is the algorithm for performing the conversion:

1. The rightmost digit of *n* is *n % b*. Push this digit onto the stack.

2. Replace *n* with *n / b*.

3. Repeat steps 1 and 2 until *n = 0* and there are no significant digits remaining.

4. Build the converted number string by popping the stack until the stack is empty.

 This algorithm will work only with bases 2 through 9.

We can implement this algorithm very easily using a stack in JavaScript. Here is the definition of a function for converting a number to any of the bases 2 through 9:

```
function mulBase(num, base) {
    var s = new Stack();
    do {
        s.push(num % base);
        num = Math.floor(num /= base);
    } while (num > 0);
    var converted = "";
    while (s.length() > 0) {
        converted += s.pop();
    }
    return converted;
}
```

Example 4-3 demonstrates how to use this function for base 2 and base 8 conversions.

Example 4-3. Converting numbers to base 2 and base 8

```
load("Stack.js");

function mulBase(num, base) {
    var s = new Stack();
    do {
        s.push(num % base);
        num = Math.floor(num /= base);
    } while (num > 0);
    var converted = "";
    while (s.length() > 0) {
        converted += s.pop();
    }
    return converted;
}

var num = 32;
var base = 2;
var newNum = mulBase(num, base);
print(num + " converted to base " + base + " is " + newNum);
num = 125;
base = 8;
var newNum = mulBase(num, base);
print(num + " converted to base " + base + " is " + newNum);
```

The output from Example 4-3 is:

```
32 converted to base 2 is 100000
125 converted to base 8 is 175
```

Palindromes

A palindrome is a word, phrase, or number that is spelled the same forward and backward. For example, "dad" is a palindrome; "racecar" is a palindrome; "A man, a plan, a canal: Panama" is a palindrome if you take out the spaces and ignore the punctuation; and 1,001 is a numeric palindrome.

We can use a stack to determine whether or not a given string is a palindrome. We take the original string and push each character onto a stack, moving from left to right. When the end of the string is reached, the stack contains the original string in reverse order, with the last letter at the top of the stack and the first letter at the bottom of the stack, as shown in Figure 4-2.

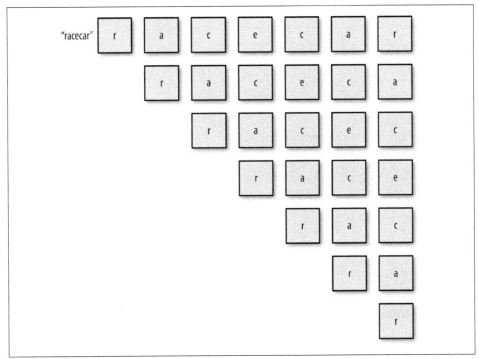

Figure 4-2. Using a stack to determine if a word is a palindrome

Once the complete original string is on the stack, we can create a new string by popping each letter the stack. This process will create the original string in reverse order. We then simply compare the original string with the reversed work, and if they are equal, the string is a palindrome.

Example 4-4 presents a program, minus the Stack class code, that determines if a given string is a palindrome.

Example 4-4. Determining if a string is a palindrome

```
load ("Stack.js");
```

```
function isPalindrome(word) {
   var s = new Stack();
   for (var i = 0; i < word.length; ++i) {
      s.push(word[i]);
   }
   var rword = "";
   while (s.length() > 0) {
      rword += s.pop();
   }
   if (word == rword) {
      return true;
    }
   else {
      return false;
   }
}

var word = "hello";
if (isPalindrome(word)) {
   print(word + " is a palindrome.");
}
else {
   print(word + " is not a palindrome.");
}
word = "racecar"
if (isPalindrome(word)) {
   print(word + " is a palindrome.");
}
else {
   print(word + " is not a palindrome.");
}
```

The output from this program is:

```
hello is not a palindrome.
racecar is a palindrome.
```

Demonstrating Recursion

Stacks are often used in the implementation of computer programming languages. One area where stacks are used is in implementing recursion. It is beyond the scope of this book to demonstrate exactly how stacks are used to implement recursive procedures, but we can use stacks to simulate recursive processes. If you are interested in learning more about recursion, a good starting point is this web page that actually uses JavaScript to describe how recursion works (*http://bit.ly/1enDGE3*).

To demonstrate how recursion is implemented using a stack, let's consider a recursive definition of the factorial function. First, here is a definition of factorial for the number 5:

$5! = 5 * 4 * 3 * 2 * 1 = 120$

Here is a recursive function to compute the factorial of any number:

```
function factorial(n) {
   if (n === 0) {
      return 1;
   }
   else {
      return n * factorial(n-1);
   }
}
```

When called with the argument 5, the function returns 120.

To simulate computing *5!* using a stack, first push the numbers 5 through 1 onto a stack. Then, inside a loop, pop each number and multiply the number by the running product, resulting in the correct answer, 120. Example 4-5 contains the code for the function, along with a test program.

Example 4-5. Simulating recursive processes using a stack

```
load("Stack.js");

function factorial(n) {
   if (n === 0) {
      return 1;
   }
   else {
      return n * factorial(n-1);
   }
}

function fact(n) {
   var s = new Stack();
   while (n > 1) {
      s.push(n--);
   }
   var product = 1;
   while (s.length() > 0) {
      product *= s.pop();
   }
   return product;
}

print(factorial(5)); // displays 120
print(fact(5)); // displays 120
```

Exercises

1. A stack can be used to ensure that an arithmetic expression has balanced paren-theses. Write a function that takes an arithmetic expression as an argument and

returns the postion in the expression where a parenthesis is missing. An example of an arithmetic expression with unbalanced parentheses is 2.3 + .

2. A postfix expression evaluator works on arithmetic expressions taking the following form:

   op1 op2 operator

   Using two stacks—one for the operands and one for the operators—design and implement a JavaScript function that converts infix expressions to postfix expressions, and then use the stacks to evaluate the expression.

3. An example of a real-world stack is a Pez dispenser. Imagine that your virtual Pez dispenser is filled with red, yellow, and white colors and you don't like the yellow ones. Write a program that uses a stack (and maybe more than one) to remove the yellow ones without changing the order of the other candies in the dispenser.

CHAPTER 5

Queues

A *queue* is a type of list where data are inserted at the end and are removed from the front. Queues are used to store data in the order in which they occur, as opposed to a stack, in which the last piece of data entered is the first element used for processing. Think of a queue like the line at your bank, where the first person into the line is the first person served, and as more customers enter a line, they wait in the back until it is their turn to be served.

A queue is an example of a first-in, first-out (FIFO) data structure. Queues are used to order processes submitted to an operating system or a print spooler, and simulation applications use queues to model scenarios such as customers standing in the line at a bank or a grocery store.

Queue Operations

The two primary operations involving queues are inserting a new element into a queue and removing an element from a queue. The insertion operation is called *enqueue*, and the removal operation is called *dequeue*. The enqueue operation inserts a new element at the end of a queue, and the dequeue operation removes an element from the front of a queue. Figure 5-1 illustrates these operations.

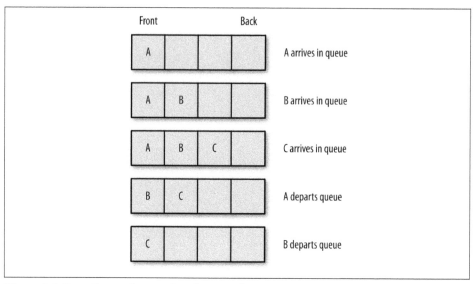

Figure 5-1. Inserting and removing elements from a queue

Another important queue operation is viewing the element at the front of a queue. This operation is called peek. The peek operation returns the element stored at the front of a queue without removing it from the queue. Besides examining the front element, we also need to know how many elements are stored in a queue, which we can satisfy with the length property; and we need to be able to remove all the elements from a queue, which is performed with the clear operation.

An Array-Based Queue Class Implementation

Implementing the Queue class using an array is straightforward. Using JavaScript arrays is an advantage many other programming languages don't have because JavaScript contains a function for easily adding data to the end of an array, push(), and a function for easily removing data from the front of an array, shift().

The push() function places its argument at the first open position of an array, which will always be the back of the array, even when there are no other elements in the array. Here is an example:

```
names = [];
name.push("Cynthia");
names.push("Jennifer");
print(names); // displays Cynthia,Jennifer
```

Then we can remove the element from the front of the array using shift():

```
names.shift();
print(names); // displays Jennifer
```

Now we're ready to begin implementing the Queue class by defining the constructor function:

```
function Queue() {
   this.dataStore = [];
   this.enqueue = enqueue;
   this.dequeue = dequeue;
   this.front = front;
   this.back = back;
   this.toString = toString;
   this.empty = empty;
}
```

The enqueue() function adds an element to the end of a queue:

```
function enqueue(element) {
   this.dataStore.push(element);
}
```

The dequeue() function removes an element from the front of a queue:

```
function dequeue() {
   return this.dataStore.shift();
}
```

We can examine the front and back elements of a queue using these functions:

```
function front() {
   return this.dataStore[0];
}
```

```
function back() {
   return this.dataStore[this.dataStore.length-1];
}
```

We also need a toString() function to display all the elements in a queue:

```
function toString() {
   var retStr = "";
   for (var i = 0; i < this.dataStore.length; ++i) {
      retStr += this.dataStore[i] + "\n";
   }
   return retStr;
}
```

Finally, we need a function that lets us know if a queue is empty:

```
function empty() {
   if (this.dataStore.length === 0) {
      return true;
   }
   else {
      return false;
   }
}
```

Example 5-1 presents the complete Queue class definition along with a test program.

Example 5-1. Queue class definition and a test program

```
function Queue() {
   this.dataStore = [];
   this.enqueue = enqueue;
   this.dequeue = dequeue;
   this.front = front;
   this.back = back;
   this.toString = toString;
   this.empty = empty;
}

function enqueue(element) {
   this.dataStore.push(element);
}

function dequeue() {
   return this.dataStore.shift();
}

function front() {
   return this.dataStore[0];
}

function back() {
   return this.dataStore[this.dataStore.length-1];
}

function toString() {
   var retStr = "";
   for (var i = 0; i < this.dataStore.length; ++i) {
      retStr += this.dataStore[i] + "\n";
   }
   return retStr;
}

function empty() {
   if (this.dataStore.length === 0) {
      return true;
   }
   else {
      return false;
   }
}

// test program

var q = new Queue();
q.enqueue("Meredith");
q.enqueue("Cynthia");
```

```
q.enqueue("Jennifer");
print(q.toString());
q.dequeue();
print(q.toString());
print("Front of queue: " + q.front());
print("Back of queue: " + q.back());
```

The output from Example 5-1 is:

```
Meredith
Cynthia
Jennifer

Cynthia
Jennifer

Front of queue: Cynthia
Back of queue: Jennifer
```

Using the Queue Class: Assigning Partners at a Square Dance

As we mentioned earlier, queues are often used to simulate situations when people have to wait in line. Once scenario we can simulate with a queue is a square dance for singles. When men and women arrive at this square dance, they enter the dance hall and stand in the line for their gender. As room becomes available on the dance floor, dance partners are chosen by taking the first man and woman in line. The next man and woman move to the front of their respective lines. As dance partners move onto the dance floor, their names are announced. If a couple leaves the floor and there is not both a man and a woman at the front of each line, this fact is announced.

This simulation will store the names of the men and women participating in the square dance in a text file. Here is the file we will use for the simulation:

```
F Allison McMillan
M Frank Opitz
M Mason McMillan
M Clayton Ruff
F Cheryl Ferenback
M Raymond Williams
F Jennifer Ingram
M Bryan Frazer
M David Durr
M Danny Martin
F Aurora Adney
```

Each dancer is stored in a Dancer object:

```
function Dancer(name, sex) {
    this.name = name;
```

```
        this.sex = sex;
    }
```

Next we need a function to load the dancers from the file into the program:

```
function getDancers(males, females) {
    var names = read("dancers.txt").split("\n");
    for (var i = 0; i < names.length; ++i) {
        names[i] = names[i].trim();
    }
    for (var i = 0; i < names.length; ++i) {
        var dancer = names[i].split(" ");
        var sex = dancer[0];
        var name = dancer[1];
        if (sex == "F") {
            females.enqueue(new Dancer(name, sex));
        }
        else {
            males.enqueue(new Dancer(name, sex));
        }
    }
}
```

The names are read from the text file into an array. The function then trims the new-line character from each line. The second loop splits each line into a two-element array, by sex and by name. Then the function examines the sex element and assigns the dancer to the appropriate queue.

The next function pairs up the male and female dancers and announces the pairings:

```
function dance(males, females) {
    print("The dance partners are: \n");
    while (!females.empty() && !males.empty()) {
        person = females.dequeue();
        putstr("Female dancer is: " + person.name);
        person = males.dequeue();
        print(" and the male dancer is: " + person.name);
    }
    print();
}
```

Example 5-2 presents all the preceding functions, as well as a test program and the Queue class.

Example 5-2. A square dance simulation

```
function Queue() {
    this.dataStore = [];
    this.enqueue = enqueue;
    this.dequeue = dequeue;
    this.front = front;
    this.back = back;
```

```
      this.toString = toString;
      this.empty = empty;
}

function enqueue(element) {
   this.dataStore.push(element);
}

function dequeue() {
   return this.dataStore.shift();
}

function front() {
   return this.dataStore[0];
}

function back() {
   return this.dataStore[this.dataStore.length-1];
}

function toString() {
   var retStr = "";
   for (var i = 0; i < this.dataStore.length; ++i) {
      retStr += this.dataStore[i] + "\n";
   }
   return retStr;
}

function empty() {
   if (this.dataStore.length == 0) {
      return true;
   }
   else {
      return false;
   }
}

function Dancer(name, sex) {
   this.name = name;
   this.sex = sex;
}

function getDancers(males, females) {
   var names = read("dancers.txt").split("\n");
   for (var i = 0; i < names.length; ++i) {
      names[i] = names[i].trim();
   }
   for (var i = 0; i < names.length; ++i) {
      var dancer = names[i].split(" ");
      var sex = dancer[0];
      var name = dancer[1];
      if (sex == "F") {
```

```
            femaleDancers.enqueue(new Dancer(name, sex));
        }
        else {
            maleDancers.enqueue(new Dancer(name, sex));
        }
    }
}

function dance(males, females) {
    print("The dance partners are: \n");
    while (!females.empty() && !males.empty()) {
        person = females.dequeue();
        putstr("Female dancer is: " + person.name);
        person = males.dequeue();
        print(" and the male dancer is: " + person.name);
    }
    print();
}

// test program

var maleDancers = new Queue();
var femaleDancers = new Queue();
getDancers(maleDancers, femaleDancers);
dance(maleDancers, femaleDancers);
if (!femaleDancers.empty()) {
    print(femaleDancers.front().name + " is waiting to dance.");
}
if (!maleDancers.empty()) {
    print(maleDancers.front().name + " is waiting to dance.");
}
```

The output from Example 5-2 is:

```
The dance partners are:

Female dancer is: Allison and the male dancer is: Frank
Female dancer is: Cheryl and the male dancer is: Mason
Female dancer is: Jennifer and the male dancer is: Clayton
Female dancer is: Aurora and the male dancer is: Raymond

Bryan is waiting to dance.
```

One change we might want to make to the program is to display the number of male
and female dancers waiting to dance. We don't have a function that displays the number of elements in a queue, so we need to add it to the Queue class definition:

```
function count() {
    return this.dataStore.length;
}
```

Be sure to add the following line to the Queue class constructor function:

```
    this.count = count;
```

In Example 5-3, we change the test program to use this new function.

Example 5-3. Providing a count of dancers waiting to dance

```
var maleDancers = new Queue();
var femaleDancers = new Queue();
getDancers(maleDancers, femaleDancers);
dance(maleDancers, femaleDancers);
if (maleDancers.count() > 0) {
    print("There are " + maleDancers.count() +
          " male dancers waiting to dance.");
}
if (femaleDancers.count() > 0) {
    print("There are " + femaleDancers.count() +
          " female dancers waiting to dance.");
}
```

When we run Example 5-3, we get the following:

```
Female dancer is: Allison and the male dancer is: Frank
Female dancer is: Cheryl and the male dancer is: Mason
Female dancer is: Jennifer and the male dancer is: Clayton
Female dancer is: Aurora and the male dancer is: Raymond

There are 3 male dancers waiting to dance.
```

Sorting Data with Queues

Queues are not only useful for simulations; they can also be used to sort data. Back in the old days of computing, programs were entered into a mainframe program via punch cards, with each card holding a single program statement. The cards were sorted using a mechanical sorter that utilized bin-like structures to hold the cards. We can simulate this process by using a set of queues. This sorting technique is called a *radix sort* (see Data Structures with C++ [Prentice Hall]). It is not the fastest of sorting algorithms, but it does demonstrate an interesting use of queues.

The radix sort works by making two passes over a data set, in this case the set of integers from 0 to 99. The first pass sorts the numbers based on the 1s digit, and the second pass sorts the numbers based on the 10s digit. Each number is placed in a bin based on the digit in each of these two places. Given these numbers:

```
91, 46, 85, 15, 92, 35, 31, 22
```

the first pass of the radix sort results in the following bin configuration:

```
Bin 0:
Bin 1: 91, 31
Bin 2: 92, 22
```

```
Bin 3:
Bin 4:
Bin 5: 85, 15, 35
Bin 6: 46
Bin 7:
Bin 8:
Bin 9:
```

Now the numbers are sorted based on which bin they are in:

```
91, 31, 92, 22, 85, 15, 35, 46
```

Next, the numbers are sorted by the 10s digit into the appropriate bins:

```
Bin 0:
Bin 1: 15
Bin 2: 22
Bin 3: 31, 35
Bin 4: 46
Bin 5:
Bin 6:
Bin 7:
Bin 8: 85
Bin 9: 91, 92
```

Finally, take the numbers out of the bins and put them back into a list, and you get the following sorted list of integers:

```
15, 22, 31, 35, 46, 85, 91, 92
```

We can implement this algorithm by using queues to represent the bins. We need nine queues, one for each digit. We will store the queues in an array. We uses the modulus and integer division operations for determining the 1s and 10s digits. The remainder of the algorithm entails adding numbers to their appropriate queues, taking the numbers out of the queues to re-sort them based on the 1s digit, and the repeating the process for the 10s digit. The result is a sorted set of integers.

First, here is the function that distributes numbers by the place (1s or 10s) digit:

```
function distribute(nums, queues, n, digit) { // digit represents either the 1s
                                               // or 10s place
   for (var i = 0; i < n; ++i) {
      if (digit == 1) {
         queues[nums[i]%10].enqueue(nums[i]);
      }
      else {
         queues[Math.floor(nums[i] / 10)].enqueue(nums[i]);
      }
   }
}
```

Here is the function for collecting numbers from the queues:

```
function collect(queues, nums) {
    var i = 0;
    for (var digit = 0; digit < 10; ++digit) {
        while (!queues[digit].empty()) {
            nums[i++] = queues[digit].dequeue();
        }
    }
}
```

Example 5-4 presents a complete program for performing a radix sort, along with a function for displaying the contents of an array.

Example 5-4. Performing a radix sort

```
function distribute(nums, queues, n, digit) {
    for (var i = 0; i < n; ++i) {
        if (digit == 1) {
            queues[nums[i]%10].enqueue(nums[i]);
        }
        else {
            queues[Math.floor(nums[i] / 10)].enqueue(nums[i]);
        }
    }
}

function collect(queues, nums) {
    var i = 0;
    for (var digit = 0; digit < 10; ++digit) {
        while (!queues[digit].empty()) {
            nums[i++] = queues[digit].dequeue();
        }
    }
}

function dispArray(arr) {
    for (var i = 0; i < arr.length; ++i) {
        putstr(arr[i] + " ");
    }
}


// main program

var queues = [];
for (var i = 0; i < 10; ++i) {
    queues[i] = new Queue();
}
var nums = [];
for (var i = 0; i < 10; ++i) {
    nums[i] = Math.floor(Math.floor(Math.random() * 101));
}
print("Before radix sort: ");
```

```
dispArray(nums);
distribute(nums, queues, 10, 1);
collect(queues, nums);
distribute(nums, queues, 10, 10);
collect(queues, nums);
print("\n\nAfter radix sort: ");
dispArray(nums);
```

Here are a couple of runs of the program:

```
Before radix sort:
45 72 93 51 21 16 70 41 27 31

After radix sort:
16 21 27 31 41 45 51 70 72 93

Before radix sort:
76 77 15 84 79 71 69 99 6 54

After radix sort:
6 15 54 69 71 76 77 79 84 99
```

Priority Queues

In the course of normal queue operations, when an element is removed from a queue, that element is always the first element that was inserted into the queue. There are certain applications of queues, however, that require that elements be removed in an order other than first-in, first-out. When we need to simulate such an application, we need to create a data structure called a *priority queue*.

A priority queue is one where elements are removed from the queue based on a priority constraint. For example, the waiting room at a hospital's emergency department (ED) operates using a priority queue. When a patient enters the ED, he or she is seen by a triage nurse. This nurse's job is to assess the severity of the patient's condition and assign the patient a priorty code. Patients with a high priority code are seen before patients with a lower priority code, and patients that have the same priority code are seen on a first-come, first-served, or first-in, first-out, basis.

Let's begin building a priority queue system by first defining an object that will store the elements of the queue:

```
function Patient(name, code) {
    this.name = name;
    this.code = code;
}
```

The value for code will be an integer that represents the patient's priority, or severity.

Now we need to redefine the dequeue() function that removes the element in the queue with the highest priority. We will define the highest priority element as being the element with the lowest code. This new `dequeue()` function will move through the queue's underlying array and find the element with the lowest code. Then the function uses the `splice()` function to remove this element. Here is the new definition for `dequeue()`:

```
function dequeue() {
    var entry = 0;
    for (var i = 0; i < this.dataStore.length; ++i) {
        if (this.dataStore[i].code < this.dataStore[entry].code) {
            entry = i;
        }
    }
    return this.dataStore.splice(entry,1);
}
```

The `dequeue()` function uses a simple sequential search to find the element with the highest priority code (the lowest number; 1 has a higher priority than 10). The function returns an array of one element—the one removed from the queue.

Finally, we add a `toString()` function modified to handle `Patient` objects:

```
function toString() {
    var retStr = "";
    for (var i = 0; i < this.dataStore.length; ++i) {
        retStr += this.dataStore[i].name + " code: "
                + this.dataStore[i].code + "\n";
    }
    return retStr;
}
```

Example 5-5 demonstrates how the priority queue system works.

Example 5-5. A priority queue implementation

```
// enqueue patients
var ed = new Queue();

var p = new Patient("Smith",5);
ed.enqueue(p);

p = new Patient("Jones", 4);
ed.enqueue(p);

p = new Patient("Fehrenbach", 6);
ed.enqueue(p);

p = new Patient("Brown", 1);
ed.enqueue(p);

p = new Patient("Ingram", 1);
ed.enqueue(p);
```

```
// print queue
print(ed.toString());

// first round
seen = ed.dequeue();
print("Patient being treated: " + seen[0].name);
print("Patients waiting to be seen: ");
print(ed.toString());

// second round
seen = ed.dequeue();
print("Patient being treated: " + seen[0].name);
print("Patients waiting to be seen: ");
print(ed.toString());

// third round
seen = ed.dequeue();
print("Patient being treated: " + seen[0].name);
print("Patients waiting to be seen: ");
print(ed.toString());

// fourth
seen = ed.dequeue();
print("Patient being treated: " + seen[0].name);
print("Patients waiting to be seen: ");
print(ed.toString());
```

Example 5-5 generates the following output:

```
"Smith code: 5
Jones code: 4
Fehrenbach code: 6
Brown code: 1
Ingram code: 1"

"Patient being treated: Brown"
"Patients waiting to be seen: "
"Smith code: 5
Jones code: 4
Fehrenbach code: 6
Ingram code: 1"

"Patient being treated: Ingram"
"Patients waiting to be seen: "
"Smith code: 5
Jones code: 4
Fehrenbach code: 6"

"Patient being treated: Jones"
"Patients waiting to be seen: "
"Smith code: 5
Fehrenbach code: 6"
```

```
"Patient being treated: Smith"
"Patients waiting to be seen: "
"Fehrenbach code: 6"
```

Exercises

1. Modify the Queue class to create a Deque class. A deque is a queue-like structure that allows elements to be added and removed from both the front and the back of the list. Test your class in a program.

2. Use the Deque class you created in Example 5-1 to determine if a given word is a palindrome.

3. Modify the priority queue example from Example 5-5 so that the higher-priority elements have higher numbers rather than lower numbers. Test your implementation with the example in the chapter.

4. Modify the ED example (Example 5-5) so the user can control the activity in the ED. Create a menu system that allows the user to choose from the following activities:

   a. Patient enters ED.

   b. Patient is seen by doctor.

   c. Display list of patients waiting to be seen.

CHAPTER 6

Linked Lists

In Chapter 3 we discussed the use of lists for storing data. The underlying data storage mechanism we use for lists is the array. In this chapter we'll discuss a different type of list, the *linked list*. We'll explain why linked lists are sometimes preferred to arrays, and we'll develop an object-based, linked-list implementation. We'll end the chapter with several examples of how linked lists can solve many programming problems you will encounter.

Shortcomings of Arrays

There are several reasons arrays are not always the best data structure to use for organizing data. In many programming languages, arrays are fixed in length, so it is hard to add new data when the last element of the array is reached. Adding and removing data from an array is also difficult because you have to move array elements up or down to reflect either an addition or a deletion. However, these problems do not come up with JavaScript arrays, since we can use the split() function without having to perform additional array element accesses.

The main problem with using JavaScript arrays, however, is that arrays in JavaScript are implemented as objects, causing them to be less efficient than arrays built in languages such as C++ and Java (see Crockford, Chapter 6).

When you determine that the operations performed on an array are too slow for practical use, you can consider using the linked list as an alternative data structure. The linked list can be used in almost every situation where a one-dimensional array is used, except when you need random access to the elements of a list. When random access is required, an array is the better data structure to use.

Linked Lists Defined

A linked list is a collection of objects called *nodes*. Each node is linked to a successor node in the list using an object reference. The reference to another node is called a *link*. An example of a linked list is shown in Figure 6-1.

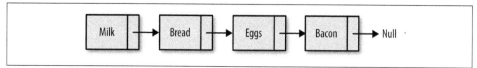

Figure 6-1. A linked list

While array elements are referenced by their position, linked list elements are referenced by their relationship to the other elements of the linked list. In Figure 6-1, we say that "bread" follows "milk", not that "bread" is in the second position. Moving through a linked list involves following the links of the list from the beginning node to the end node (not including the header node, which is sometimes used as a hook for entry into a linked list). Something else to notice in the figure is that we mark the end of a linked list by pointing to a null node.

Marking the beginning of a linked list can be a problem. Many linked-list implementations include a special node, called the *head*, to denote the beginning of a linked list. The linked list shown in Figure 6-1 is redesigned in Figure 6-2 to include a head node.

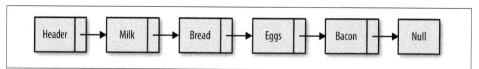

Figure 6-2. A linked list with a head node

Inserting a new node into a linked list is a very efficient task. To insert a new node, the link of the node before the inserted node (the *previous* node) is changed to point to the new node, and the new node's link is set to the node the previous node was pointing to before the insertion. Figure 6-3 illustrates how "cookies" is added to the linked list after "eggs."

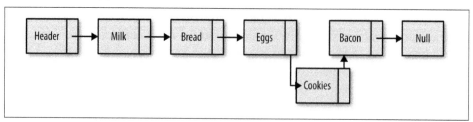

Figure 6-3. Inserting "cookies" into the linked list

Removing an item from a linked list is also easy to do. The link of the node before the removed node is redirected to point to the node the removed node is pointing to, while also pointing the removed node to null, effectively taking the node out of the linked list. Figure 6-4 shows how "bacon" is removed from the linked list.

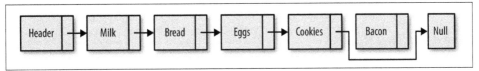

Figure 6-4. Removing "bacon" from the linked list

There are other functions we can perform with a linked list, but insertion and removal are the two functions that best describe why linked lists are so useful.

An Object-Based Linked List Design

Our design of a linked list will involve creating two classes. We'll create a Node class for adding nodes to a linked list, and we'll create a LinkedList class, which will provide functions for inserting nodes, removing nodes, displaying a list, and other housekeeping functions.

The Node Class

The Node class consists of two properties: element, which store's the node's data, and next, which stores a link to the next node in the linked list. To create nodes, we'll use a constructor function that sets the values for the two properties:

```
function Node(element) {
    this.element = element;
    this.next = null;
}
```

The Linked List Class

The LList class provides the functionality for a linked list. The class includes functions for inserting new nodes, removing nodes, and finding a particular data value in a list. There is also a constructor function used for creating a new linked list. The only property stored in a linked list is a node to represent the head of the list.

Here is the definition for the constructor function:

```
function LList() {
    this.head = new Node("head");
    this.find = find;
    this.insert = insert;
    this.remove = remove;
```

```
        this.display = display;
    }
```

The head node starts with its next property set to null and is changed to point to the first element inserted into the list, since we create a new Node element but don't modify its next property here in the constructor.

Inserting New Nodes

The first function we'll examine is the insert function, which inserts a node into a list. To insert a new node, you have to specify which node you want to insert the new node before or after. We'll start by demonstrating how to insert a new node after an existing node.

To insert a node after an existing node, we first have to find the "after" node. To do this, we create a helper function, find(), which searches through the linked list looking for the specified data. When this data is found, the function returns the node storing the data. Here is the code for the find() function:

```
function find(item) {
    var currNode = this.head;
    while (currNode.element != item) {
        currNode = currNode.next;
    }
    return currNode;
}
```

The find() function demonstrates how to move through a linked list. First, we create a new node and assign it as the head node. Then we loop through the linked list, moving from one node to the next when the value of the current node's element property is not equal to the data we are searching for. If the search is successful, the function returns the node storing the data. If the data is not found, the function returns null.

Once the "after" node is found, the new node is inserted into the linked list. First, the new node's next property is set to the value of the next property of the "after" node. Then the "after" node's next property is set to a reference to the new node. Here is the definition of the insert() function:

```
function insert(newElement, item) {
    var newNode = new Node(newElement);
    var current = this.find(item);
    newNode.next = current.next;
    current.next = newNode;
}
```

We're ready now to test our linked list code. However, before we do that, we need a function that will display the elements of a linked list. The display() function is defined below:

```
function display() {
    var currNode = this.head;
    while (!(currNode.next === null)) {
        print(currNode.next.element);
        currNode = currNode.next;
    }
}
```

This function starts by hooking into the linked list by assigning the head of the list to a new node. We then loop through the linked list, only stopping when the value of the current node's next property is set to null. In order to display only nodes with data in them (in other words, not the head node), we access the element property of the node that the current node is pointing to:

```
currNode.next.element
```

Finally, we need to add some code to use the linked list. Example 6-1 contains a short program that sets up a linked list of cities in western Arkansas that are located on Interstate 40, along with the complete LList class definition up to this point. Notice that the remove() function is commented out. It will be defined in the next section.

Example 6-1. The LList class and a test program

```
function LList() {
    this.head = new Node("head");
    this.find = find;
    this.insert = insert;
    //this.remove = remove;
    this.display = display;
}

function find(item) {
    var currNode = this.head;
    while (currNode.element != item) {
        currNode = currNode.next;
    }
    return currNode;
}

function insert(newElement, item) {
    var newNode = new Node(newElement);
    var current = this.find(item);
    newNode.next = current.next;
    current.next = newNode;
}

function display() {
    var currNode = this.head;
    while (!(currNode.next === null)) {
        print(currNode.next.element);
        currNode = currNode.next;
```

```
    }
}

// main program

var cities = new LList();
cities.insert("Conway", "head");
cities.insert("Russellville", "Conway");
cities.insert("Alma", "Russellville");
cities.display();
```

The output from Example 6-1 is:

```
Conway
Russellville
Alma
```

Removing Nodes from a Linked List

In order to remove a node from a linked list, we need to find the node that is just before the node we want to remove. Once we find that node, we change its next property to no longer reference the removed node, and the previous node is modified to point to the node after the removed node. We can define a function, findPrevious(), to perform this task. This function traverses the linked list, stopping at each node to see if the next node stores the data that is to be removed. When the data is found, the function returns this node (the "previous" node), so that its next property can be modified. Here is the definition for findPrevious():

```
function findPrevious(item) {
   var currNode = this.head;
   while (!(currNode.next === null) &&
          (currNode.next.element != item)) {
      currNode = currNode.next;
   }
   return currNode;
}
```

Now we're ready to write the remove() function:

```
function remove(item) {
   var prevNode = this.findPrevious(item);
   if (!(prevNode.next == null)) {
       prevNode.next = prevNode.next.next;
   }
}
```

The main line of code in this function looks odd, but makes perfect sense:

```
prevNode.next = prevNode.next.next
```

We are just skipping over the node we want to remove and linking the "previous" node with the node just after the one we are removing. Refer back to Figure 6-4 if you need help visualizing this operation.

We are ready to test our code again, but first we need to modify the constructor function for the LList class to include these new functions:

```
function LList() {
    this.head = new Node("head");
    this.find = find;
    this.insert = insert;
    this.display = display;
    this.findPrevious = findPrevious;
    this.remove = remove;
}
```

Example 6-2 provides a short program that tests the remove() function:

Example 6-2. Testing the remove() function

```
var cities = new LList();
cities.insert("Conway", "head");
cities.insert("Russellville", "Conway");
cities.insert("Carlisle", "Russellville");
cities.insert("Alma", "Carlisle");
cities.display();
print();
cities.remove("Carlisle");
cities.display();
```

The output from Example 6-2 before the removal is:

```
Conway
Russellville
Carlisle
Alma
```

But Carlisle is in eastern Arkansas, so we need to remove it from the list, resulting in the following output:

```
Conway
Russellville
Alma
```

Example 6-3 contains a complete listing of the Node class, the LList class, and our test program:

Example 6-3. The Node class and the LList class

```
function Node(element) {
    this.element = element;
```

```
      this.next = null;
   }

   function LList() {
      this.head = new Node("head");
      this.find = find;
      this.insert = insert;
      this.display = display;
      this.findPrevious = findPrevious;
      this.remove = remove;
   }

   function remove(item) {
      var prevNode = this.findPrevious(item);
      if (!(prevNode.next === null)) {
         prevNode.next = prevNode.next.next;
      }
   }

   function findPrevious(item) {
      var currNode = this.head;
      while (!(currNode.next === null) &&
            (currNode.next.element != item)) {
         currNode = currNode.next;
      }
      return currNode;
   }

   function display() {
      var currNode = this.head;
      while (!(currNode.next === null)) {
         print(currNode.next.element);
         currNode = currNode.next;
      }
   }

   function find(item) {
      var currNode = this.head;
      while (currNode.element != item) {
         currNode = currNode.next;
      }
      return currNode;
   }

   function insert(newElement, item) {
      var newNode = new Node(newElement);
      var current = this.find(item);
      newNode.next = current.next;
      current.next = newNode;
   }
```

```
var cities = new LList();
cities.insert("Conway", "head");
cities.insert("Russellville", "Conway");
cities.insert("Carlisle", "Russellville");
cities.insert("Alma", "Carlisle");
cities.display();
print();
cities.remove("Carlisle");
cities.display();
```

Doubly Linked Lists

Although traversing a linked list from the first node to the last node is straightforward, it is not as easy to traverse a linked list backward. We can simplify this procedure if we add a property to our Node class that stores a link to the previous node. When we insert a node into the list, we'll have to perform more operations to assign the proper links for the next and previous nodes, but we gain efficiency when we have to remove a node from the list, since we no longer have to search for the previous node. Figure 6-5 illustrates how a doubly linked list works.

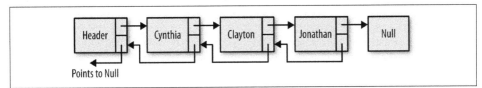

Figure 6-5. A doubly linked list

Our first task is to assign a `previous` property to our Node class:

```
function Node(element) {
    this.element = element;
    this.next = null;
    this.previous = null;
}
```

The `insert()` function for a doubly linked list is similar to the `insert()` function for the singly linked list, except that we have to set the new node's `previous` property to point to the previous node. Here is the definition:

```
function insert(newElement, item) {
    var newNode = new Node(newElement);
    var current = this.find(item);
    newNode.next = current.next;
    newNode.previous = current;
    current.next = newNode;
}
```

The `remove()` function for a doubly linked list is more efficient than for a singly linked list because we don't have to find the previous node. We first need to find the node in the list that is storing the data we want to remove. Then we set that node's `previous` property to the node pointed to by the deleted node's `next` property. Then we need to redirect the `previous` property of the node the deleted node points to and point it to the node before the deleted node. Figure 6-6 makes this situation easier to understand.

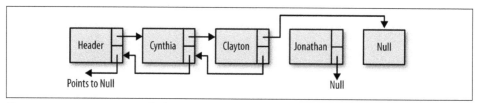

Figure 6-6. Removing a node from a doubly linked list

Here is the code for the `remove()` function:

```
function remove(item) {
   var currNode = this.find(item);
   if (!(currNode.next === null)) {
      currNode.previous.next = currNode.next;
      currNode.next.previous = currNode.previous;
      currNode.next = null;
      currNode.previous = null;
   }
}
```

In order to perform tasks such as displaying a linked list in reverse order, we can use a utility function that finds the last node in a doubly linked list. The following function, `findLast()`, moves us to the last node of a list without going past the end of the list:

```
function findLast() {
   var currNode = this.head;
   while (!(currNode.next === null)) {
      currNode = currNode.next;
   }
   return currNode;
}
```

With the `findLast()` function written, we can write a function to display the elements of a doubly linked list in reverse order. Here is the code for the `dispReverse()` function:

```
function dispReverse() {
   var currNode = this.head;
   currNode = this.findLast();
   while (!(currNode.previous === null)) {
      print(currNode.element);
      currNode = currNode.previous;
   }
}
```

The last task to accomplish is to add these new functions to the constructor function for the doubly linked list class. Example 6-4 presents this code, along with the rest of the code for implementing a doubly linked list, as well as a short program to test the code.

Example 6-4. The LList *class as a doubly linked list*

```
function Node(element) {
    this.element = element;
    this.next = null;
    this.previous = null;
}

function LList() {
    this.head = new Node("head");
    this.find = find;
    this.insert = insert;
    this.display = display;
    this.remove = remove;
    this.findLast = findLast;
    this.dispReverse = dispReverse;
}

function dispReverse() {
    var currNode = this.head;
    currNode = this.findLast();
    while (!(currNode.previous === null)) {
        print(currNode.element);
        currNode = currNode.previous;
    }
}

function findLast() {
    var currNode = this.head;
    while (!(currNode.next === null)) {
        currNode = currNode.next;
    }
    return currNode;
}

function remove(item) {
    var currNode = this.find(item);
    if (!(currNode.next === null)) {
        currNode.previous.next = currNode.next;
        currNode.next.previous = currNode.previous;
        currNode.next = null;
        currNode.previous = null;
    }
}

// findPrevious is no longer needed
```

```
/*function findPrevious(item) {
    var currNode = this.head;
    while (!(currNode.next === null) &&
            (currNode.next.element != item)) {
       currNode = currNode.next;
    }
    return currNode;
}*/

function display() {
    var currNode = this.head;
    while (!(currNode.next === null)) {
       print(currNode.next.element);
       currNode = currNode.next;
    }
}

function find(item) {
    var currNode = this.head;
    while (currNode.element != item) {
       currNode = currNode.next;
    }
    return currNode;
}

function insert(newElement, item) {
    var newNode = new Node(newElement);
    var current = this.find(item);
    newNode.next = current.next;
    newNode.previous = current;
    current.next = newNode;
}


var cities = new LList();
cities.insert("Conway", "head");
cities.insert("Russellville", "Conway");
cities.insert("Carlisle", "Russellville");
cities.insert("Alma", "Carlisle");
cities.display();
print();
cities.remove("Carlisle");
cities.display();
print();
cities.dispReverse();
```

The output from Example 6-4 is:

```
Conway
Russellville
Carlisle
Alma
```

```
Conway
Russellville
Alma

Alma
Russellville
Conway
```

Circularly Linked Lists

A circularly linked list is similar to a singly linked list and has the same type of nodes. The only difference is that a circularly linked list, when created, has its head node's next property point back to itself. This means that the assignment:

```
head.next = head
```

is propagated throughout the circularly linked list so that every new node has its next property pointing to the head of the list. In other words, the last node of the list is always pointing back to the head of the list, creating a circular list, as shown in Figure 6-7.

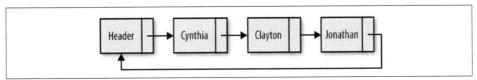

Figure 6-7. A circularly linked list

The reason you might want to create a circularly linked list is if you want the ability to go backward through a list but don't want the extra overhead of creating a doubly linked list. You can move backward through a circularly linked list by moving forward through the end of the list to the node you are trying to reach.

To create a circularly linked list, change the constructor function of the LList class to read:

```
function LList() {
    this.head = new Node("head");
    this.head.next = this.head;
    this.find = find;
    this.insert = insert;
    this.display = display;
    this.findPrevious = findPrevious;
    this.remove = remove;
}
```

This is the only change we have to make in order to make a singly linked list into a circularly linked list. However, some of the other linked list functions will not work correctly unmodified. For example, one function that needs to be modified is dis play(). As written, if the display() function is executed on a circularly linked list, the function will never stop. The condition of the while loop needs to change so that the head element is tested for and the loop will stop when it gets to the head.

Here is how the display() function is written for a circularly linked list:

```
function display() {
    var currNode = this.head;
    while (!(currNode.next === null) &&
           !(currNode.next.element == "head")) {
        print(currNode.next.element);
        currNode = currNode.next;
    }
}
```

Seeing how to modify the display() function, you should be able to modify other functions from a standard linked list to make them work with a circularly linked list.

Other Linked List Functions

There are several other functions you might include in order to have a well-functioning linked list. In the upcoming exercises, you will have the opportunity to develop some of these functions, including:

advance(n)
>   Advances *n* nodes in the linked list

back(n)
>   Moves *n* nodes backward in a doubly linked list

show()
>   Displays the current node only

Exercises

1. Implement the advance(n) function so that when executed, the current node is moved *n* nodes forward in the list.

2. Implement the back(n) function so that when executed, the current node is moved *n* spaces backward in the list.

3. Implement the show() function, which displays the data associated with the current node.

4. Write a program that uses a singly linked list to keep track of a set of test grades entered interactively into the program.

5. Rewrite your solution to Example 6-4 using a doubly linked list.

6. According to legend, the first-century Jewish historian Flavius Josephus was about to be captured along with a band of 40 compatriots by Roman soldiers during the Jewish-Roman War. The Jewish soldiers decided that they preferred suicide to being captured and devised a plan for their demise. They were to form a circle and kill every third soldier until they were all dead. Josephus and one other decided they wanted no part of this and quickly calculated where they needed to place themselves so they would be the last survivors. Write a program that allows you to place *n* people in a circle and specify that every *m*th person will be killed. The program should determine the number of the last two people left in the circle. Use a circularly linked list to solve the problem.

CHAPTER 7

Dictionaries

A dictionary is a data structure that stores data as *key-value* pairs, such as the way a phone book stores its data as names and phone numbers. When you look for a phone number, you first search for the name, and when you find the name, the phone number is found right next to the name. The key is the element you use to perform a search, and the value is the result of the search.

The JavaScript Object class is designed to operate as a dictionary. In this chapter we'll use the features of the Object class to build a Dictionary class that simplifies working with a dictionary-type object. You can perform the same functions shown in this chapter using just JavaScript arrays and objects, but creating a Dictionary class makes doing the work easier and more fun. For example, it's a lot easier to use () to reference keys rather than having to use [ ] notation. There is also, of course, the advantage of being able to define functions for performing collective operations, such as displaying all entries in a dictionary, rather than having to write loops in the main program to perform the same operations.

The Dictionary Class

The basis for the Dictionary class is an Object, but using Array access notation, since objects in JavaScript are *associative arrays..* This approach allows us to dynamically add key-value pairs, and use Array functionality such as sorting, but at the same time, allowing us to have string keys rather than just numeric.

We'll start our definition of the Dictionary class with this code:

```
function Dictionary() {
    this.datastore = {};
}
```

The first function to define is add(). This function takes two arguments, a key and a value. The key is the index for the value element. Here is the code:

```
function add(key, value) {
        this.datastore[key] = value;
}
```

Next, we define the find() function. This function takes a key as its argument and returns the value associated with it. The code looks like this:

```
function find(key) {
        return this.datastore[key];
}
```

Removing a key-value pair from a dictionary involves using a built-in JavaScript function: delete. This function is part of the Object class and takes a reference to a key as its argument. The function deletes both the key and the associated value. Here is the definition of our remove() function:

```
function remove(key) {
        delete this.datastore[key];
}
```

Finally, we'd like to be able to view all the key-value pairs in a dictionary, so here is a function that accomplishes this task:

```
function showAll() {
    for (var key in this.datastore) {
        print(key + " -> " + this.datastore[key]);
    }
}
```

Example 7-1 provides the definition of the Dictionary class up to this point.

Example 7-1. The Dictionary class

```
function Dictionary() {
    this.add = add;
    this.datastore = {};
    this.find = find;
    this.remove = remove;
    this.showAll = showAll;
}

function add(key, value) {
    this.datastore[key] = value;
}

function find(key) {
    return this.datastore[key];
}
```

```
function remove(key) {
   delete this.datastore[key];
}

function showAll() {
   for (var key in this.datastore) {
      print(key + " -> " + this.datastore[key]);
   }
}
```

A program that uses the Dictionary class is shown in Example 7-2.

Example 7-2. Using the Dictionary class

```
load("dictionary.js");
var pbook = new Dictionary();
pbook.add("Mike","123");
pbook.add("David", "345");
pbook.add("Cynthia", "456");
print("David's extension: " + pbook.find("David"));
pbook.remove("David");
pbook.showAll();
```

The output from this program is:

```
David's extension: 345
Mike -> 123
Cynthia -> 456
```

Auxiliary Functions for the Dictionary Class

We can define several functions that can help in special situations. For example, it is nice to know how many entries there are in a dictionary. Here is a count() function definition:

```
function count() {
   var n = 0;
   for (var key in this.datastore) {
      ++n;
   }
   return n;
}
```

You might be wondering why the length property wasn't used for the count() function. The reason is that length doesn't work with an object, even one being accessed using array functionality. The use of string keys precludes some Array object functionality. For example:

```
var nums = [];
nums[0] = 1;
```

```
    nums[1] = 2;
    print(nums.length); // displays 2
    var pbook = [];
    pbook["David"] = 1;
    pbook["Jennifer"] = 2;
    print(pbook.length); // displays 0
```

Another helper function we can use is a clear() function. Here's the definition:

```
    function clear() {
       for (var key in this.datastore) {
          delete this.datastore[key];
       }
    }
```

Example 7-3 updates the complete Dictionary class definition.

Example 7-3. Updated Dictionary class definition

```
function Dictionary() {
   this.add = add;
   this.datastore = {};
   this.find = find;
   this.remove = remove;
   this.showAll = showAll;
   this.count = count;
   this.clear = clear;
}

function add(key, value) {
    this.datastore[key] = value;
}

function find(key) {
        return this.datastore[key];
}

function remove(key) {
        delete this.datastore[key];
}

function showAll() {
   for (var key in this.datastore) {
      print(key + " -> " + this.datastore[key]);
   }
}

function count() {
   var n = 0;
   for (var key in this.datastore) {
      ++n;
   }
```

```
    return n;
}

function clear() {
    for (var key in this.datastore) {
        delete this.datastore[key];
    }
}
```

Example 7-4 illustrates how these new auxiliary functions work.

Example 7-4. Using the count() *and* clear() *functions*

```
load("dictionary.js");
var pbook = new Dictionary();
pbook.add("Raymond","123");
pbook.add("David", "345");
pbook.add("Cynthia", "456");
print("Number of entries: " + pbook.count());
print("David's extension: " + pbook.find("David"));
pbook.showAll();
pbook.clear();
print("Number of entries: " + pbook.count());
```

The output from this code is:

```
Number of entries: 3
David's extension: 345
Raymond -> 123
David -> 345
Cynthia -> 456
Number of entries: 0
```

Adding Sorting to the Dictionary Class

The primary purpose of a dictionary is to retrieve a value by referencing its key. The actual order that the dictionary items are stored in is not a primary concern. However, many people like to see a listing of a dictionary in sorted order. Let's see what it takes to display our dictionary items in sorted order.

Arrays can be sorted. For example:

```
var a = [];
a[0] = "Mike";
a[1] = "David";
print(a); // displays Mike,David
a.sort();
print(a); // displays David,Mike
```

We can't perform the same test with string keys, however. The output from the program is empty. This is much the same problem we had earlier trying to define a count() function.

This isn't really a problem, however. All that matters to the user of the class is that when the dictionary's contents are displayed, the results are in sorted order. We can use the Object.keys() function to solve this problem. Here is a new definition for the showAll() function:

```
function showAll() {
  var keys = Object.keys(this.datastore);
  keys.sort();
  for (var i = 0; i < keys.length; i++) {
    print(keys[i] + " -> " + this.datastore[keys[i]]);
  }

}
```

The only difference between this definition of the function and our earlier definition is we've added a call to sort() after we obtain the keys from the datastore array via the Object.keys() function. Example 7-5 demonstrates how this new function definition is used to display a sorted list of names and numbers.

Example 7-5. A sorted dictionary display

```
load("dictionary2.js");
var pbook = new Dictionary();
pbook.add("Raymond","123");
pbook.add("David", "345");
pbook.add("Cynthia", "456");
pbook.add("Mike", "723");
pbook.add("Jennifer", "987");
pbook.add("Danny", "012");
pbook.add("Jonathan", "666");
pbook.showAll();
```

Here is the output of the program:

```
Cynthia -> 456
Danny -> 012
David -> 345
Jennifer -> 987
Jonathan -> 666
Mike -> 723
Raymond -> 123
```

Exercises

1. Write a program that takes a set of names and phone numbers from a text file and stores them in a Dictionary object. Include in your program the ability to display one phone number, display all phone numbers, add new phone numbers, remove phone numbers, and clear out the list of numbers.

2. Using the Dictionary class, write a program that stores the number of occurrences of words in a text. Your program should display each word in a text just once as well as the number of times the word occurs in the text. For example, given the text "the brown fox jumped over the blue fox," the output will be:

   ```
   the: 2
   brown: 1
   fox: 2
   jumped: 1
   over: 1
   blue: 1
   ```

3. Rewrite exercise 2 so that it displays the words in sorted order.

CHAPTER 8

Hashing

Hashing is a common technique for storing data in such a way that the data can be inserted and retrieved very quickly. Hashing uses a data structure called a *hash table*. Although hash tables provide fast insertion, deletion, and retrieval, they perform poorly for operations that involve searching, such as finding the minimum and maximum values in a data set. For these operations, other data structures such as the binary search tree are more appropriate. We'll learn how to implement a hash table in this chapter and learn when it's appropriate to use hashing as a data storage and retrieval technique.

An Overview of Hashing

The hash table data structure is designed around an array. The array consists of elements 0 through some predetermined size, though we can increase the size when necessary. Each data element is stored in the array based on an associated data element called the *key*, which is similar to the concept of the key we examined with the dictionary data structure. To store a piece of data in a hash table, the key is mapped into a number in the range of 0 through the hash table size, using a *hash function*.

Ideally, the hash function stores each key in its own array element. However, because there are an unlimited number of possible keys and a limited number of array elements (theoretical in JavaScript), a more realistic goal of the hash function is to attempt to distribute the keys as evenly as possible among the elements of the array.

Even with an efficient hash function, it is possible for two keys to hash (the result of the hash function) to the same value. This is called a *collision*, and we need a strategy for handling collisions when they occur. We'll discuss how to deal with collisions in detail later in the chapter.

The last thing we have to determine when creating a hash function is how large an array to create for the hash table. One constraint usually placed on the array size is that it should be a prime number. We will explain why this number should be prime when we examine the different hash functions. After that, there are several different strategies for determining the correct array size, all of them based on the technique used to handle collisions, so we will examine this issue when we discuss handling collisions. Figure 8-1 illustrates the concept of hashing using the example of a small phone book.

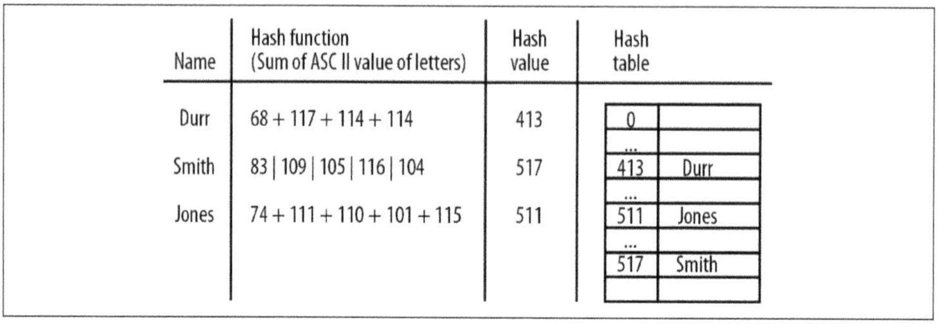

Name	Hash function (Sum of ASC II value of letters)	Hash value	Hash table	
Durr	68 + 117 + 114 + 114	413	0	
			...	
Smith	83 | 109 | 105 | 116 | 104	517	413	Durr
			...	
Jones	74 + 111 + 110 + 101 + 115	511	511	Jones
			...	
			517	Smith

Figure 8-1. Hashing names and telephone numbers

A Hash Table Class

We need a class to represent the hash table. The class will include functions for computing hash values, a function for inserting data into the hash table, a function for retrieving data from the hash table, and a function for displaying the distribution of data in the hash table, as well as various utility functions we might need.

Here is the constructor function for our HashTable class:

```
function HashTable() {
    this.table = new Array(137);
    this.simpleHash = simpleHash;
    this.showDistro = showDistro;
    this.put = put;
    //this.get = get;
}
```

The get() function is commented out for now; we'll describe its definition later in the chapter.

Choosing a Hash Function

The choice of a hash function depends on the data type of the key. If your key is an integer, then the simplest hash function is to return the key modulo the size of the array. There are circumstances when this function is not recommended, such as when the keys all end in 0 and the array size is 10. This is one reason the array size should always be a prime number, such as 137, which is the value we used in the preceding constructor function. Also, if the keys are random integers, then the hash function should more evenly distribute the keys. This type of hashing is known as *modular hashing*.

In many applications, the keys are strings. Choosing a hash function to work with string keys proves to be more difficult and should be chosen carefully.

A simple hash function that at first glance seems to work well is to sum the ASCII value of the letters in the key. The hash value is then that sum modulo the array size. Here is the definition for this simple hash function:

```
function simpleHash(data) {
    var total = 0;
    for (var i = 0; i < data.length; ++i) {
        total += data.charCodeAt(i);
    }
    return total % this.table.length;
}
```

We can finish up this first attempt at the HashTable class with definitions for put() and showDistro(), which place the data in the hash table and display the data from the hash table respectively. Here is the complete class definition:

```
function HashTable() {
    this.table = new Array(137);
    this.simpleHash = simpleHash;
    this.showDistro = showDistro;
    this.put = put;
    //this.get = get;
}

function put(data) {
    var pos = this.simpleHash(data);
    this.table[pos] = data;
}

function simpleHash(data) {
    var total = 0;
    for (var i = 0; i < data.length; ++i) {
        total += data.charCodeAt(i);
    }
    return total % this.table.length;
}

function showDistro() {
    var n = 0;
    for (var i = 0; i < this.table.length; ++i) {
        if (this.table[i] != undefined) {
            print(i + ": " + this.table[i]);
```

```
        }
      }
    }
```

Example 8-1 demonstrates how the simpleHash() function works.

Example 8-1. Hashing using a simple hash function

```
load("HashTable.js");
var someNames = ["David", "Jennifer", "Donnie", "Raymond",
                "Cynthia", "Mike", "Clayton", "Danny", "Jonathan"];
var hTable = new HashTable();
for (var i = 0; i < someNames.length; ++i) {
   hTable.put(someNames[i]);
}
hTable.showDistro();
```

Here is the output from Example 8-1:

```
35: Cynthia
45: Clayton
57: Donnie
77: David
95: Danny
116: Mike
132: Jennifer
134: Jonathan
```

The simpleHash() function computes a hash value by summing the ASCII value of each name using the JavaScript function charCodeAt() to return a character's ASCII value. The put() function receives the array index value from the simpleHash() function and stores the data element in that position. The showDistro() function displays where the names are actually placed into the array using the hash function. As you can see, the data is not particularly evenly distributed. The names are bunched up at the beginning and at the end of the array.

There is an even bigger problem than just the uneven distribution of names in the array, however. If you pay close attention to the output, you'll see that not all the names in the original array of names are displayed. Let's investigate further by adding a print() statement to the simpleHash() function:

```
function simpleHash(data) {
   var total = 0;
   for (var i = 0; i < data.length; ++i) {
      total += data.charCodeAt(i);
   }
   print("Hash value: " + data + " -> " + total);
   return total % this.table.length;
}
```

When we run the program again, we see the following output:

```
Hash value: David -> 488
Hash value: Jennifer -> 817
Hash value: Donnie -> 605
Hash value: Raymond -> 730
Hash value: Cynthia -> 720
Hash value: Mike -> 390
Hash value: Clayton -> 730
Hash value: Danny -> 506
Hash value: Jonathan -> 819
35: Cynthia
45: Clayton
57: Donnie
77: David
95: Danny
116: Mike
132: Jennifer
134: Jonathan
```

The problem is now apparent—the strings "Clayton" and "Raymond" hash to the same value, causing a collision. Because of the collision, only "Clayton" is stored in the hash table. We can improve our hash function to avoid such collisions, as discussed in the next section.

A Better Hash Function

To avoid collisions, you first need to make sure the array you are using for the hash table is sized to a prime number. This is necessary due to the use of modular arithmetic in computing the key. The size of the array needs to be greater than 100 in order to more evenly disperse the keys in the table. Through experimentation, we found that the first prime number greater than 100 that didn't cause collisions for the data set used in Example 8-1 is 137. When smaller prime numbers close to 100 were used, there were still collisions in the data set.

After properly sizing the hash table, the next step to avoiding hashing collisions is to compute a better hash value. An algorithm known as Horner's method does the trick. Without getting too deep into the mathematics of the algorithm, our new hash function still works by summing the ASCII values of the characters of a string, but it adds a step by multiplying the resulting total by a prime constant. Most algorithm textbooks suggest a small prime number, such as 31, which worked without collisions with our test data set.

We now present a new, better hash function utilizing Horner's method:

```
function betterHash(string, arr) {
   var H = 31;
   var total = 0;
   for (var i = 0; i < string.length; ++i) {
      total += H * total + string.charCodeAt(i);
   }
}
```

```
      total = total % arr.length;
      return parseInt(total);
   }
```

Example 8-2 contains the current definition of the HashTable class.

Example 8-2. The HashTable class with the betterHash() function

```
function HashTable() {
   this.table = new Array(137);
   this.simpleHash = simpleHash;
   this.betterHash = betterHash;
   this.showDistro = showDistro;
   this.put = put;
   //this.get = get;
}

function put(data) {
   var pos = this.betterHash(data);
   this.table[pos] = data;
}

function simpleHash(data) {
   var total = 0;
   for (var i = 0; i < data.length; ++i) {
      total += data.charCodeAt(i);
   }
   print("Hash value: " + data + " -> " + total);
   return total % this.table.length;
}

function showDistro() {
   var n = 0;
   for (var i = 0; i < this.table.length; ++i) {
      if (this.table[i] !== undefined) {
         print(i + ": " + this.table[i]);
      }
   }
}

function betterHash(string) {
   var H = 31;
   var total = 0;
   for (var i = 0; i < string.length; ++i) {
      total += H * total + string.charCodeAt(i);
   }
   total = total % this.table.length;
   if (total < 0) {
      total += this.table.length-1;
   }
   return parseInt(total);
}
```

Notice that the put() function is now using betterHash() rather than simpleHash().

The program in Example 8-3 tests our new hash function.

Example 8-3. Testing the betterHash() function

```
load("betterhash.js");
var someNames = ["David", "Jennifer", "Donnie", "Raymond",
                "Cynthia", "Mike", "Clayton", "Danny", "Jonathan"];
var hTable = new HashTable();
for (var i = 0; i < someNames.length; ++i) {
   hTable.put(someNames[i]);
}
hTable.showDistro();
```

The result of running this program is:

```
3: David
25: Raymond
37: Donnie
61: Jonathan
75: Danny
82: Mike
102: Jennifer
130: Clayton
131: Cynthia
```

All nine names are now present and accounted for.

Hashing Integer Keys

In the last section we worked with string keys. In this section, we introduce how to hash integer keys. The data set we're working with is student grades. The key is a nine-digit student identification number, which we will generate randomly, along with the student's grade. Here are the functions we use to generate the student data (ID and grade):

```
function getRandomInt (min, max) {
    return Math.floor(Math.random() * (max - min + 1)) + min;
}

function genStuData(arr) {
    for (var i = 0; i < arr.length; ++i) {
        var num = "";
        for (var j = 1; j <= 9; ++j) {
            num += Math.floor(Math.random() * 10);
        }
        num += getRandomInt(50, 100);
        arr[i] = num;
    }
}
```

The getRandomInt() function allows us to specify a maximum and minimum random number. For a set of student grades, it is reasonable to say that the minimum grade is 50 and the maximum grade is 100.

The getStuData() function generates student data. The inner loop generates the student ID number, and right after the inner loop finishes, a random grade is generated and concatenated to the student ID. Our main program will separate the ID from the grade. The hash function will total the individual digits in the student ID to compute a hash value using the simpleHash() function.

Example 8-4 presents a program that uses the original Hash Table functionality and new functions to store a set of students and their grades.

Example 8-4. Hashing integer keys

```
function getRandomInt (min, max) {
    return Math.floor(Math.random() * (max - min + 1)) + min;
}

function genStuData(arr) {
    for (var i = 0; i < arr.length; ++i) {
        var num = "";
        for (var j = 1; j <= 9; ++j) {
            num += Math.floor(Math.random() * 10);
        }
        num += getRandomInt(50,100);
        arr[i] = num;
    }
}

load("HashTable.js");
var numStudents = 10;
var arrSize = 97;
var idLen = 9;
var students = new Array(numStudents);
genStuData(students);
print ("Student data: \n");
for (var i = 0; i < students.length; ++i) {
    print(students[i].substring(0,8) + " " +
        students[i].substring(9));
}
print("\n\nData distribution: \n");
var hTable = new HashTable();
for (var i = 0; i < students.length; ++i) {
    hTable.put(students[i]);
}
hTable.showDistro();
```

The output from Example 8-4 is:

```
Student data:

45337671 91
97949453 89
83030638 82
10682591 78
05789018 86
76750339 85
16627331 84
82500333 62
04734766 95
00848878 65


Data distribution:

15: 82500333362
24: 16627331384
26: 83030638582
30: 45337671491
35: 04734766495
36: 00848878265
37: 76750339485
50: 97949453389
```

Once again, our hash function creates a collision, and not all of the data is stored in the array. Actually, if you run the program several times, all of the data will sometimes get stored, but the results are far from consistent. We can play around with array sizes to see if we can fix the problem, or we can simply change the hash function called by the put() function and use betterHash(). When using betterHash() with the student data, we get the following output:

```
Student data:

88793345 50
95713806 51
41222483 98
89264661 66
46867539 81
75890255 82
10989115 81
42498519 52
29731650 73
00514025 55


Data distribution:

18: 46867539781
51: 10989115081
63: 42498519652
90: 00514025355
```

```
101: 88793345350
123: 75890255682
127: 89264661866
129: 95713806451
133: 29731650173
135: 41222483698
```

The lesson here is obvious: betterHash() is the superior hashing function for strings and for integers.

Storing and Retrieving Data in a Hash Table

Now that we've covered hash functions, we can apply this knowledge to use a hash table to actually store data. To do this, we have to modify the put() function so that it accepts both a key and data, hashes the key, and then uses that information to store the data in the table. Here is the definition of the new put() function:

```
function put(key, data) {
    var pos = this.betterHash(key);
    this.table[pos] = data;
}
```

The put() function hashes the key and then stores the data in the position of the table computed by the hash function.

Next we need to define the get() function so that we can retrieve data stored in a hash table. This function must, again, hash the key so that it can determine where the data is stored, and then retrieve the data from its position in the table. Here is the definition:

```
function get(key) {
    return this.table[this.betterHash(key)];
}
```

Here is a program to test the put() and get() functions:

```
load("betterhash2.js");
var pnumbers = new HashTable();
var name, number;
while (name != "finished") {
    putstr("Enter a name (or 'finished' when done): ");
    name = readline();
    if (name == "finished") {
        break;
    }
    putstr("Enter a number: ");
    number = readline();
    pnumbers.put(name, number);
}
name = "";
putstr("Name for number (Enter quit to stop): ");
while (name != "quit") {
```

```
    name = readline();
    if (name == "quit") {
        break;
    }
    print(name + "'s number is " + pnumbers.get(name));
    putstr("Name for number (Enter quit to stop): ");
}
```

This program allows you to enter names and numbers until you type in *finished* and will retrieve numbers based on names until you tell the program to quit.

Handling Collisions

A collision occurs when a hash function generates the same key for two or more values. The second part of a hash algorithm involves resolving collisions so that all keys are stored in the hash table. In this section, we look at two means of collision resolution: *separate chaining* and *linear probing*.

Separate Chaining

When a collision occurs, we still need to be able to store the key at the generated index, but it is physically impossible to store more than one piece of data in an array element. Separate chaining is a technique where each array element of a hash table stores another data structure, such as another array, which is then used to store keys. Using this technique, if two keys generate the same hash value, each key can be stored in a different position of the secondary array. Figure 8-2 illustrates how separate chaining works.

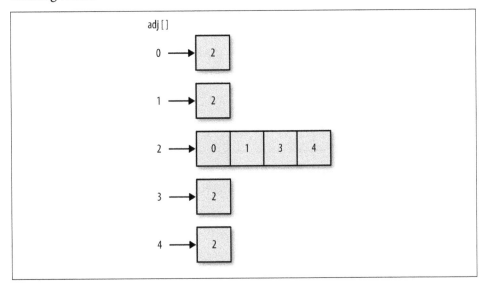

Figure 8-2. Separate chaining

To implement separate chaining, after we create the array to store the hashed keys, we call a function that assigns an empty array to each array element of the hash table. This creates a two-dimensional array (see Chapter 3 for an explantion of two-dimenstional arrays). The following code defines a function, buildChains(), to create the second array (we'll also refer to this array as a *chain*), as well as a small program that demonstrates how to use buildChains():

```
function buildChains() {
    for (var i = 0; i < this.table.length; ++i) {
        this.table[i] = [];
    }
}
```

Add the preceding code, along with a declaration of the function, to the definition of the HashTable class.

In order to properly display the distribution after hashing with separate chaining, we need to modify the showDistro() function in the following way to recognize that the hash table is now a multidimensional array:

```
function showDistro() {
    var n = 0;
    for (var i = 0; i < this.table.length; ++i) {
        if (this.table[i][0] !== undefined) {
            print(i + ": " + this.table[i]);
        }
    }
}
```

Next we need to define the put() and get() functions that will work with separate chaining. The put() function hashes the key and then attempts to store the data in the first cell of the chain at the hashed position. If that cell already has data in it, the function searches for the first open cell and stores the data in that cell. Here is the code for the put() function:

```
function put(data) {
    var key = this.betterHash(data);
    var index = 0;
    if (this.table[key][index] == undefined) {
        this.table[key][index] = data;
    }
    else {
        while (this.table[key][index] !== undefined) {
            ++index;
        }
        this.table[key][index] = data;
    }
}
```

Unlike the example earlier when we were just storing keys, this put() function has to store both keys and values. The function uses a pair of the chain's cells to store a key-value pair; the first cell stores the key and the adjacent cell of the chain stores the value.

The get() function starts out by hashing the key to get the position of the key in the hash table. Then the function searches the cells until it finds the key it is looking for. When it finds the correct key, it returns the data from the adjacent cell to the key's cell. If the key is not found, the function returns undefined. Here is the code:

```
function get(key) {
    var index = 0;
    var pos = this.betterHash(key);
    if (this.table[pos][index] == key) {
        return this.table[pos][index+1];
    }
    else {
        while (this.table[pos][index] != key) {
            index += 2;
        }
        return this.table[pos][index+1];
    }
    return undefined;
}
```

A program to test separate chaining is shown in Example 8-5. The loop to load the names is run twice to deliberately create collisions based on the key, which is then handled by the chaining.

Example 8-5. Using separate chaining to avoid collisions

```
load("separatechain.js");
var hTable = new HashTable();
hTable.buildChains();
var someNames = ["David", "Jennifer", "Donnie", "Raymond",
                 "Cynthia", "Mike", "Clayton", "Danny", "Jonathan"];
for (var i = 0; i < someNames.length; ++i) {
    hTable.put(someNames[i]);
}
for (var i = 0; i < someNames.length; ++i) {
    hTable.put(someNames[i]);
}

hTable.showDistro();
```

When we run the program in Example 8-5, we get the following output:

```
 3: David,David
25: Raymond,Raymond
37: Donnie,Donnie
61: Jonathan,Jonathan
75: Danny,Danny
82: Mike,Mike
```

```
102: Jennifer,Jennifer
130: Clayton,Clayton
131: Cynthia,Cynthia
```

Linear Probing

A second technique for handling collisions is called *linear probing*. Linear probing is an example of a more general hashing technique called *open-addressing hashing*. With linear probing, when there is a collision, the program simply looks to see if the next element of the hash table is empty. If so, the key is placed in that element. If the element is not empty, the program continues to search for an empty hash-table element until one is found. This technique makes use of the fact that any hash table is going to have many empty elements and it makes sense to use the space to store keys.

Linear probing should be chosen over separate chaining when your array for storing data can be fairly large. Here's a formula commonly used to determine which collision method to use: if the size of the array can be up to half the number of elements to be stored, you should use separate chaining; but if the size of the array can be twice the size of the number of elements to be stored, you should use linear probing.

To demonstrate how linear probing works, we can rewrite the put() and get() functions to work with linear probing. In order to create a realistic data-retrieval system, we have to modify the HashTable class by adding a second array to store values. The table array and the values array work in parallel, so that when we store a key in a position in the tables array, we store a value in the corresponding position in the values array.

Add the following code to the HashTable constructor:

```
this.values = [];
```

Now we can define the put() method for linear probing:

```
function put(key, data) {
   var pos = this.betterHash(key);
   if (this.table[pos] === undefined) {
      this.table[pos] = key;
      this.values[pos] = data;
   }
   else {
      while (this.table[pos] !== undefined) {
         pos++;
      }
      this.table[pos] = key;
      this.values[pos] = data;
   }
}
```

The code for the get() function begins searching the hash table at the hashed position of the key. If the data passed to the function matches the key found at that position, the corresponding data in the values position is returned. If the keys don't match, the function loops through the hash table until it either finds the key or reaches a cell that is undefined, meaning the key was never placed into the hash table. Here's the code:

```
function get(key) {
    var hash = -1;
    hash = this.betterHash(key);
    if (hash > -1) {
        for (var i = hash; this.table[hash] !== undefined; i++) {
            if (this.table[hash] == key) {
                return this.values[hash];
            }
        }
    }
    return undefined;
}
```

Exercises

1. Use linear probing to create a simple dictionary to store the definitions of words. Your program should have two parts. The first part reads a text file that contains a list of words and definitions and stores them in a hash table. The second part of the program allows a user to enter a word and see the definition of that word.

2. Repeat exercise 1 using separate chaining.

3. Write a program using hashing that reads a text file and compiles a list of the words in the file with the number of times each word appears in the file.

CHAPTER 9

Sets

A set is a collection of unique elements. The elements of a set are called members. The two most important properties of sets are that the members of a set are unordered and that no member can occur in a set more than once. Sets play a very important role in computer science but are not considered a data type in many programming languages. Sets can be useful when you want to create a data structure that consists only of unique elements, such as a list of each unique word in a text. This chapter discusses how to create a Set class for JavaScript.

Fundamental Set Definitions, Operations, and Properties

A set is an unordered collection of related members in which no member occurs more than once. A set is denoted mathematically as a list of members surrounded by curly braces, such as {0,1,2,3,4,5,6,7,8,9}. We can write a set in any order, so the previous set can be written as {9,0,8,1,7,2,6,3,5,4} or any other combination of the members such that all the members are written just once.

Set Definitions

Here are some definitions you need to know to work with sets:

- A set containing no members is called the *empty set*. The *universe* is the set of all possible members.
- Two sets are considered equal if they contain exactly the same members.
- A set is considered a *subset* of another set if all the members of the first set are contained in the second set.

Set Operations

The fundamental operations performed on sets are:

Union
A new set is obtained by combining the members of one set with the members of another set.

Intersection
A new set is obtained by adding all the members of one set that also exist in a second set.

Difference
A new set is obtained by adding all the members of one set except those that also exist in a second set.

The Set Class Implementation

The Set class implementation is built around an array for storing the data. We also create functions for each of the set operations outlined above. Here is the definition for the constructor function:

```
function Set() {
    this.dataStore = [];
    this.add = add;
    this.remove = remove;
    this.size = size;
    this.union = union;
    this.intersect = intersect;
    this.subset = subset;
    this.difference = difference;
    this.show = show;
}
```

An Array is used rather than the new ECMAScript 6 Set, because Sets have limited support at this time.

Let's look at the add() function first:

```
function add(data) {
    if (this.dataStore.indexOf(data) < 0) {
        this.dataStore.push(data);
        return true;
    }
    else {
        return false;
```

```
        }
    }
```

Because a set can only contain unique members, before the add() function can store data in the array, it must check to make sure the data isn't already in the array. We use the indexOf() function to check the array for the requested data. This function returns the position of an element in an array, or the value -1 if the array doesn't contain the element. If the data isn't stored in the array, the function pushes the data onto the array and returns true. Otherwise, the function returns false. We need to write add() as a Boolean function so we have to way to know for sure whether or not the data was added to the set.

The remove() function works similarly to the add() function. We first check to see if the requested data is in the array. If it is, we call the splice() function to remove the data and return true. Otherwise, we return false, indicating the requested data isn't in the set. Here is the definition of remove():

```
function remove(data) {
    var pos = this.dataStore.indexOf(data);
    if (pos > -1) {
        this.dataStore.splice(pos,1);
        return true;
    }
    else {
        return false;
    }
}
```

Before we can test these functions, let's define the show() function so we can see the members of a set:

```
function show() {
    return this.dataStore;
}
```

Let's also comment out the Set assignments to functions that don't yet exist. Example 9-1 demonstrates how the Set class works up to now.

Example 9-1. Using the Set class

```
load("Set.js");
var names = new Set();
names.add("David");
names.add("Jennifer");
names.add("Cynthia");
names.add("Mike");
names.add("Raymond");
if (names.add("Mike")) {
    print("Mike added")
}
```

```
else {
    print("Can't add Mike, must already be in set");
}
print(names.show());
var remove = "Mike";
if (names.remove(remove)) {
    print(removed + " removed.");
}
else {
    print(remove + " not removed.");
}
names.add("Clayton");
print(names.show());
remove = "Alisa";
if (names.remove(remove)) {
    print(remove + " removed.");
}
else {
    print(remove + " not removed.");
}
```

The output from Example 9-1 is:

```
Can't add Mike, must already be in set
David,Jennifer,Cynthia,Mike,Raymond
Mike removed.
David,Jennifer,Cynthia,Raymond,Clayton
Alisa not removed.
```

More Set Operations

The more interesting functions to define are union(), intersect(), subset(), and difference(). The union() function combines two sets using the union set opera-tion to form a new set. The function first builds a new set by adding all the members of the first set. Then the function checks each member of the second set to see whether the member is already a member of the first set. If it is, the member is skip-ped over, and if not, the member is added to the new set.

Before we define union(), however, we need to define a helper function, contains(), which looks to see if a specified member is part of a set. Here is the definition for contains():

```
function contains(data) {
    if (this.dataStore.indexOf(data) > -1) {
        return true;
    }
    else {
        return false;
    }
}
```

Now we can define the union() function:

```
function union(set) {
    var tempSet = new Set();
    for (var i = 0; i < this.dataStore.length; ++i) {
        tempSet.add(this.dataStore[i]);
    }
    for (var i = 0; i < set.dataStore.length; ++i) {
        if (!tempSet.contains(set.dataStore[i])) {
            tempSet.dataStore.push(set.dataStore[i]);
        }
    }
    return tempSet;
}
```

Example 9-2 demonstrates the use of union(), after uncommenting its assignment in Set, and adding the contains helper function reference:

Example 9-2. Computing the union of two sets

```
load("Set.js");
var cis = new Set();
cis.add("Mike");
cis.add("Clayton");
cis.add("Jennifer");
cis.add("Raymond");
var dmp = new Set();
dmp.add("Raymond");
dmp.add("Cynthia");
dmp.add("Jonathan");
var it = new Set();
it = cis.union(dmp);
print(it.show());
//displays Mike,Clayton,Jennifer,Raymond,Cynthia,Jonathan
```

Set intersection is performed using a function named intersect(). This function is easier to define. Each time a member of the first set is found to be a member of the second set it is added to a new set, which is the return value of the function. Here is the definition:

```
function intersect(set) {
    var tempSet = new Set();
    for (var i = 0; i < this.dataStore.length; ++i) {
        if (set.contains(this.dataStore[i])) {
            tempSet.add(this.dataStore[i]);
        }
    }
    return tempSet;
}
```

Computing the intersection of two sets is shown in Example 9-3, after uncommenting the intersect Set property assignment.

Example 9-3. Computing the intersection of two sets

```
load("Set.js");
var cis = new Set();
cis.add("Mike");
cis.add("Clayton");
cis.add("Jennifer");
cis.add("Raymond");
var dmp = new Set();
dmp.add("Raymond");
dmp.add("Cynthia");
dmp.add("Bryan");
var inter = cis.intersect(dmp);
print(inter.show()); // displays Raymond
```

The next operation to define is subset. The subset() function first has to check to make sure that the proposed subset's length is less than the larger set we are comparing with the subset. If the subset length is greater than the original set, then it cannot be a subset. Once it is determined that the subset size is smaller, the function then checks to see that each member of the subset is a member of the larger set. If any one member of the subset is not in the larger set, the function returns false and stops. If the function gets to the end of the larger set without returning false, the subset is indeed a subset and the function returns true. The definition is below:

```
function subset(set) {
   if (this.size() > set.size()) {
      return false;
   }
   else {
      for each (var member in this.dataStore) {
         if (!set.contains(member)) {
            return false;
         }
      }
   }
   return true;
}
```

The subset() function uses the size() function before checking to see if each element of the sets match. Here is the code for the size() function:

```
function size() {
   return this.dataStore.length;
}
```

You'll notice that the subset() function uses a for each loop instead of a for loop, as we've used in the other definitions. Either loop will work here, but we just used the for each loop to show that its use is fine here.

Uncomment out both the size and subset property assignments in Set. Example 9-4 computes the subset of two sets.

Example 9-4. Computing the subset of two sets

```
load("Set.js");
var it = new Set();
it.add("Cynthia");
it.add("Clayton");
it.add("Jennifer");
it.add("Danny");
it.add("Jonathan");
it.add("Terrill");
it.add("Raymond");
it.add("Mike");
var dmp = new Set();
dmp.add("Cynthia");
dmp.add("Raymond");
dmp.add("Jonathan");
if (dmp.subset(it)) {
    print("DMP is a subset of IT.");
}
else {
    print("DMP is not a subset of IT.");
}
```

Example 9-4 displays the following output:

```
DMP is a subset of IT.
```

If we add one new member to the dmp set:

```
dmp.add("Shirley");
```

then the program displays:

```
DMP is not a subset of IT.
```

The last operational function is difference(). This function returns a set that contains those members of the first set that are not in the second set. The definition for difference() is shown below:

```
function difference(set) {
    var tempSet = new Set();
    for (var i = 0; i < this.dataStore.length; ++i) {
        if (!set.contains(this.dataStore[i])) {
            tempSet.add(this.dataStore[i]);
        }
```

```
        }
        return tempSet;
    }
```

All property assignments in Set should now be uncommented. Example 9-5 computes the difference of two sets.

Example 9-5. Computing the difference of two sets

```
load("Set.js");
var cis = new Set();
var it = new Set();
cis.add("Clayton");
cis.add("Jennifer");
cis.add("Danny");
it.add("Bryan");
it.add("Clayton");
it.add("Jennifer");
var diff = new Set();
diff = cis.difference(it);
print("[" + cis.show() + "] difference [" + it.show()
      + "] -> [" + diff.show() + "]");
```

Example 9-5 displays:

```
[Clayton,Jennifer,Danny] difference [Bryan,Clayton,Jennifer] ->
[Danny]
```

Exercises

1. Modify the Set class so that the class stores its elements in sorted order. Write a program to test your implementation.

2. Modify the Set class so that it uses a linked list to store its elements rather than an array. Write a program to test your implementation.

3. Add the function higher(element) to the Set class. This function returns the least element in the set strictly greater than the given element. Test your function in a program.

4. Add the function lower(element) to the Set class. This function returns the greatest element in the set strictly less than the given element. Test your function in a program.

CHAPTER 10

Binary Trees and Binary Search Trees

Trees are a commonly used data structure in computer science. A tree is a nonlinear data structure that is used to store data in a hierarchical manner. Tree data structures are used to store hierarchical data, such as the files in a file system, and for storing sorted lists of data. We examine one particular tree structure in this chapter: the *binary tree*. Binary trees are chosen over other more primary data structures because you can search a binary tree very quickly (as opposed to a linked list, for example) and you can quickly insert and delete data from a binary tree (as opposed to an array).

Trees Defined

A tree is made up of a set of *nodes* connected by *edges*. An example of a tree is a company's organizational chart (see Figure 10-1).

The purpose of an organizational chart is to communicate the structure of an organization. In Figure 10-1, each box is a node, and the lines connecting the boxes are the edges. The nodes represent the positions that make up an organization, and the edges represent the relationships between those positions. For example, the CIO reports directly to the CEO, so there is an edge between those two nodes. The development manager reports to the CIO, so there is an edge connecting those two positions. The VP of Sales and the development manager do not have a direct edge connecting them, so there is not a direct relationship between those two positions.

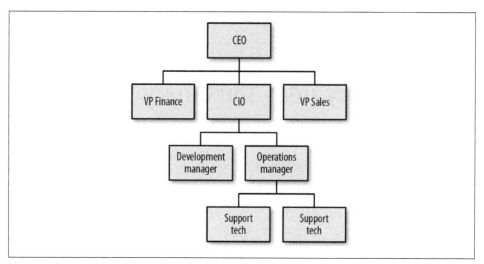

Figure 10-1. An organizational chart is a tree structure

Figure 10-2 displays another tree that defines more of the terms we need when discussing trees. The top node of a tree is called the *root* node. If a node is connected to other nodes below it, the preceding node is called the *parent* node, and the nodes following it are called *child* nodes. A node can have zero, one, or more child nodes connected to it. A node without any child nodes is called a *leaf* node.

Special types of trees, called *binary trees*, restrict the number of child nodes to no more than two. Binary trees have certain computational properties that make them very efficient for many operations. Binary trees are examined extensively in the sections to follow.

Continuing to examine Figure 10-2, you can see that by following certain edges, you can travel from one node to other nodes that are not directly connected. The series of edges you follow to get from one node to another node is called a *path*. Paths are depicted in the figure with dashed lines. Visiting all the nodes in a tree in some particular order is known as a *tree traversal*.

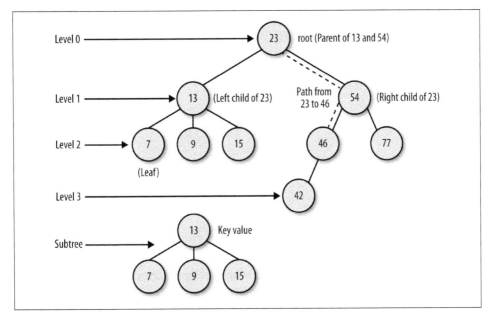

Figure 10-2. The parts of a tree

A tree can be broken down into *levels*. The root node is at level 0, its children are at level 1, those nodes' children are at level 2, and so on. A node at any level is considered the root of a *subtree*, which consists of that root node's children, its children's children, and so on. We can define the depth of a tree as the number of layers in the tree.

This concept of the root node being at the top of a tree, while in real life a tree's root is at the bottom of the tree, is counterintuitive, but it is a time-honored convention in computer science to draw trees with the root at the top. The computer scientist Donald Knuth actually tried to change the convention but gave up after a few months when he discovered that most computer scientists refused to adapt to the natural way of drawing trees.

Finally, each node in a tree has a value associated with it. This value is sometimes referred to as the *key* value.

Binary Trees and Binary Search Trees

As mentioned earlier, a *binary tree* is one where each node can have no more than two children. By limiting the number of children to two, we can write efficient programs for inserting data, searching for data, and deleting data in a tree.

Before we discuss building a binary tree in JavaScript, we need to add two terms to our tree lexicon. The child nodes of a parent node are referred to as the *left* node and the *right* node. For certain binary tree implementations, certain data values can be stored only in left nodes, and other data values must be stored in right nodes. An example binary tree is shown in Figure 10-3.

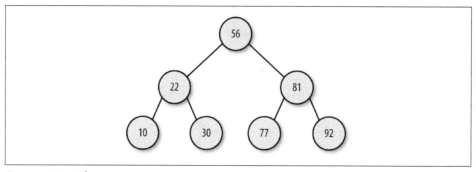

Figure 10-3. A binary tree

Identifying the child nodes is important when we consider a more specific type of binary tree, the *binary search tree*. A binary search tree is a binary tree in which data with lesser values are stored in left nodes and data with greater values are stored in right nodes. This property provides for very efficient searches and holds for both numeric data and non-numeric data, such as words and strings.

Building a Binary Search Tree Implementation

A binary search tree is made up of nodes, so the first object we need to create is a Node object, which is similar to the Node object we used with linked lists. The definition for the Node class is:

```
function Node(data, left, right) {
   this.data = data;
   this.left = left;
   this.right = right;
   this.show = show;
}

function show() {
   return this.data;
}
```

The Node object stores both data and links to other nodes (left and right). There is also a show() function for displaying the data stored in a node.

Now we can build a class to represent a binary search tree (BST). The class consists of just one data member: a Node object that represents the root node of the BST. The constructor for the class sets the root node to null, creating an empty node.

The first function we need for the BST is insert(), to add new nodes to the tree. This function is complex and requires explanation. The first step in the function is to create a Node object, passing in the data the node will store.

The second step in insertion is to check the BST for a root node. If a root node doesn't exist, then the BST is new and this node is the root node, which completes the function definition. Otherwise, the function moves to the next step.

If the node being inserted is not the root node, then we have to prepare to traverse the BST to find the proper insertion point. This process is similar to traversing a linked list. The function uses a Node object that is assigned as the current node as the function moves from level to level in the BST. The function also has to position itself inside the BST at the root node.

Once inside the BST, the next step is to determine where to put the node. This is performed inside a loop that breaks once the correct insertion point is determined. The algorithm for determining the current insertion point for a node is as follows:

1. Set the root node to be the current node.
2. If the data value in the inserted node is less than the data value in the current node, set the new current node to be the left child of the current node. If the data value in the inserted node is greater than the data value in the current node, skip to step 4.
3. If the value of the left child of the current node is null, insert the new node here and exit the loop. Otherwise, skip to the next iteration of the loop.
4. Set the current node to be the right child of the current node.
5. If the value of the right child of the current node is null, insert the new node here and exit the loop. Otherwise, skip to the next iteration of the loop.

With this algorithm complete, we're ready to implement this part of the BST class. Example 10-1 has the code for the class, including the code for the Node object.

Example 10-1. The BST and Node classes

```
function Node(data, left, right) {
    this.data = data;
    this.left = left;
    this.right = right;
    this.show = show;
}

function show() {
    return this.data;
}
```

```
function BST() {
   this.root = null;
   this.insert = insert;
   this.inOrder = inOrder;
}

function insert(data) {
   var n = new Node(data, null, null);
   if (this.root === null) {
      this.root = n;
   }
   else {
      var current = this.root;
      var parent;
      while (true) {
         parent = current;
         if (data < current.data) {
            current = current.left;
            if (current === null) {
               parent.left = n;
               break;
            }
         }
         else {
            current = current.right;
            if (current === null) {
               parent.right = n;
               break;
            }
         }
      }
   }
}
```

Traversing a Binary Search Tree

We now have the beginnings of the BST class, but all we can do is insert nodes into the tree. We need to be able to traverse the BST so that we can display the data in different orders, such as numeric or alphabetic order.

There are three traversal functions used with BSTs: *inorder*, *preorder*, and *postorder*. An inorder traversal visits all of the nodes of a BST in ascending order of the node key values. A preorder traversal visits the root node first, followed by the nodes in the subtrees under the left child of the root node, followed by the nodes in the subtrees under the right child of the root node. A postorder traversal visits all of the child nodes of the left subtree up to the root node, and then visits all of the child nodes of the right subtree up to the root node.

Although it's easy to understand why we would want to perform an inorder traversal, it is less obvious why we need preorder and postorder traversals. We'll implement all three traversal functions now and explain their uses in a later section.

The inorder traversal is best written using recursion. Since the function visits each node in ascending order, the function must visit both the left node and the right node of each subtree, following the subtrees under the left child of the root node before following the subtrees under the right child of the root. If you are unsure about using recursion, Chapter 1 discusses how to write a recursive function.

Here is the code for the inorder traversal function:

```
function inOrder(node) {
    if (node !== null) {
        inOrder(node.left);
        putstr(node.show() + " ");
        inOrder(node.right);
    }
}
```

Example 10-2 provides a short program to test the function.

Example 10-2. Inorder traversal of a BST

```
load("BSTtree.js");
var nums = new BST();
nums.insert(23);
nums.insert(45);
nums.insert(16);
nums.insert(37);
nums.insert(3);
nums.insert(99);
nums.insert(22);
print("Inorder traversal: ");
nums.inOrder(nums.root);
```

The output from Example 10-2 is:

```
Inorder traversal:
3 16 22 23 37 45 99
```

Figure 10-4 illustrates the path the inOrder() function followed.

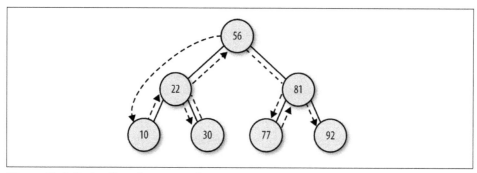

Figure 10-4. Path of inorder traversal

The definition of the preorder traversal function is:

```
function preOrder(node) {
    if (node !== null) {
        putstr(node.show() + " ");
        preOrder(node.left);
        preOrder(node.right);
    }
}
```

You'll notice that the only difference between the inOrder() and preOrder() functions is how the three lines of code inside the if statement are ordered. The call to the
show() function is sandwiched between the two recursive calls in the inOrder()
function, and the call to show() is before the two recursive calls in the preOrder()
function.

Figure 10-5 illustrates the preorder traversal path.

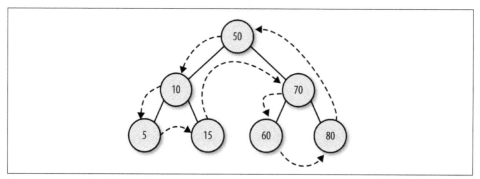

Figure 10-5. Path of preorder traversal

Add a property assignment for the new preOrder() function to BST. If we add a call
to preOrder() to the preceding program, using the same nums.root, we get the following results:

```
Inorder traversal:
3 16 22 23 37 45 99

Preorder traversal:
23 16 3 22 45 37 99
```

The path of a postorder traversal is shown in Figure 10-6.

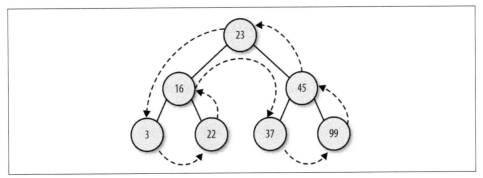

Figure 10-6. Path of postorder traversal

Here is the implementation of the postOrder() function, which is then assigned to
the BST's new postOrder property:

```
function postOrder(node) {
    if (node !== null) {
        postOrder(node.left);
        postOrder(node.right);
        putstr(node.show() + " ");
    }
}
```

And here is the output when we add the function to our program:

```
Inorder traversal:
3 16 22 23 37 45 99

Preorder traversal:
23 16 3 22 45 37 99

Postorder traversal:
3 22 16 37 99 45 23
```

We will demonstrate some practical programming examples using BSTs that make
use of these traversal functions later in the chapter.

BST Searches

There are three types of searches typically performed with a BST:

1. Searching for a specific value

2. Searching for the minimum value

3. Searching for the maximum value

We explore these three searches in the following sections.

Searching for the Minimum and Maximum Value

Searches in a BST for the minimum and maximum values stored are relatively simple procedures. Since lower values are always stored in left child nodes, to find the minimum value in a BST, you only have to traverse the left edge of the BST until you get to the last node.

Here is the definition of a function, getMin(), that finds the minimum value of a BST:

```
function getMin() {
   var current = this.root;
   while (current.left !== null) {
      current = current.left;
   }
   return current.data;
}
```

The function travels down the left link of each node in the BST until it reaches the left end of the BST, which is defined as:

```
current.left = null;
```

When this point is reached, the data stored in the current node must be the minimum value.

To find the maximum value stored in a BST, the function must simply traverse the right links of nodes until the function reaches the right end of the BST. The value stored in this node must be the maximum value.

The definition for the getMax() function is below:

```
function getMax() {
   var current = this.root;
   while (current.right !== null) {
      current = current.right;
   }
   return current.data;
}
```

Example 10-3 tests the getMin() and getMax() functions with the BST data we used earlier, after adding both to the BST object.

Example 10-3. Testing getMin() and getMax()

```
load("BSTtree.js");
var nums = new BST();
nums.insert(23);
nums.insert(45);
nums.insert(16);
nums.insert(37);
nums.insert(3);
nums.insert(99);
nums.insert(22);
var min = nums.getMin();
print("The minimum value of the BST is: " + min);
print("\n");
var max = nums.getMax();
print("The maximum value of the BST is: " + max);
```

The output from this program is:

```
The minimum value of the BST is: 3
The maximum value of the BST is: 99
```

These functions return the data stored in the minimum and maximum positions, respectively. Instead, we may want the functions to return the nodes where the minimum and maximum values are stored. To make that change, just have the functions return the current node rather than the value stored in the current node.

Searching for a Specific Value

Searching for a specific value in a BST requires that a comparison be made between the data stored in the current node and the value being searched for. The comparison will determine if the search travels to the left child node, or to the right child node if the current node doesn't store the searched-for value.

We can implement searching in a BST with the find() function, which is defined here:

```
function find(data) {
    var current = this.root;
    while (current && current.data != data) {
        if (data < current.data) {
            current = current.left;
        }
        else {
            current = current.right;
        }
    }
    return current;
}
```

This function returns the current node if the value is found in the BST and returns null if the value is not found.

Example 10-4 provides a program to test the find() function.

Example 10-4. Using find() to search for a value

```
load("BSTtree.js");
var nums = new BST();
nums.insert(23);
nums.insert(45);
nums.insert(16);
nums.insert(37);
nums.insert(3);
nums.insert(99);
nums.insert(22);
inOrder(nums.root);
print("\n");
putstr("Enter a value to search for: ");
var value = parseInt(readline());
var found = nums.find(value);
if (found !== null) {
    print("Found " + value + " in the BST.");
}
else {
    print(value + " was not found in the BST.");
}
```

The output from this program is:

```
3 16 22 23 37 45 99

Enter a value to search for: 23
Found 23 in the BST.
```

Removing Nodes from a BST

The most complex operation on a BST is removing a node. The complexity of node removal depends on which node you want to delete. If you want to remove a node with no children, the removal is fairly simple. If the node has just one child node, either left or right, the removal is a little more complex to accomplish. The removal of a node with two children is the most complex removal operation to perform.

To aid in managing the complexity of removal, we remove nodes from a BST recursively. The two functions we will define are remove() and removeNode().

The first step to take when removing a node from a BST is to check to see if the current node holds the data we are trying to remove. If so, remove that node. If not, then we compare the data in the current node to the data we are trying to remove. If the data we want to remove is less than the data in the current node, move to the left child of the current node and compare data. If the data we want to remove is greater than the data in the current node, move to the right child of the current node and compare data.

The first case to consider is when the node to be removed is a leaf (a node with no children). Then all we have to do is set the link that is pointing to the node of the parent node to null.

When the node we want to remove has one child, then the the link that is pointing to the node to be removed has to be adjusted to point to the removed node's child node.

Finally, when the node we want to remove has two children, the correct solution is to either find the largest value in the subtree to the left of the removed node, or to find the smallest value in the subtree to the right of the removed node. We will choose to go to the right.

We need a function that finds the smallest value of a subtree, getSmallest(), which we will then use to create a temporary node containing that smallest value. We copy that value into the position of the node we are replacing, and we delete the temporary node to complete the operation.

The node removal process consists of two functions. The remove() function simply receives the value to be removed and calls the second function, removeNode(), which does all the work. The definitions of the two functions are shown here:

```
function remove(data) {
    root = removeNode(this.root, data);
}

function removeNode(node, data) {
    if (node === null) {
        return null;
    }
    if (data == node.data) {
        // node has no children
        if (node.left === null && node.right === null) {
            return null;
        }
        // node has no left child
        if (node.left === null) {
            return node.right;
        }
        // node has no right child
        if (node.right === null) {
            return node.left;
        }
        // node has two children
        var tempNode = getSmallest(node.right);
        node.data = tempNode.data;
```

```
          node.right = this.removeNode(node.right, tempNode.data);
          return node;
        }
        else if (data < node.data) {
          node.left = this.removeNode(node.left, data);
          return node;
        }
        else {
          node.right = this.removeNode(node.right, data);
          return node;
        }
    }

    function getSmallest(node) {
      if (node.left == null) {
        return node;
      }
      else {
        return getSmallest(node.left);
      }
    }
```

Example 10-5 provides a program to test the remove() function, after it and remove
Node() have been added to the BST object.

Example 10-5. Using find() to search for a value

```
load("BSTtree.js");
var nums = new BST();
nums.insert(23);
nums.insert(45);
nums.insert(16);
nums.insert(37);
nums.insert(3);
nums.insert(99);
nums.insert(22);
inOrder(nums.root);
print("\n");
putstr("Enter a value to search for: ");
var value = parseInt(readline());
var found = nums.find(value);
if (found !== null) {
    print("Found " + value + " in the BST.");
}
else {
    print(value + " was not found in the BST.");
}
```

The output from this program is:

```
Inorder traversal:
3 16 22 23 37 45 99
```

```
Inorder traversal after removing 37:
3 16 22 23 45 99
```

Counting Occurrences

One use of a BST is to keep track of the occurrences of data in a data set. For example, we can use a BST to record the distribution of grades on an exam. Given a set of exam grades, we can write a program that checks to see if the grade is in the BST, adding the grade to the BST if it is not found, and incrementing the number of occurrrences of it if the grade is found in the BST.

To solve this problem, we need to modify the Node object to include a field for keeping track of the number of occurrences of a grade in the BST, and we need a function for updating a node so that if we find a grade in the BST, we can increment the occurrences field.

Let's start by modifying our definition of the Node object to include a field for keeping track of grade occurrences:

```
function Node(data, left, right) {
    this.data = data;
    this.count =   1;
    this.left = left;
    this.right = right;
    this.show = show;
}
```

When a grade (a Node object) is inserted into a BST, its count is set to 1. The BST insert() function will work fine as is, but we need to add a function to update the BST when the count field needs to be incremented. We'll call this function update():

```
function update(data) {
    var grade = this.find(data);
    grade.count++;
    return grade;
}
```

The other functions of the BST class are fine as is. We just need a couple of functions to generate a set of grades and to display the grades:

```
function prArray(arr) {
    putstr(arr[0].toString() + ' ');
    for (var i = 1; i < arr.length; ++i) {
        putstr(arr[i].toString() + ' ');
        if (i % 10 === 0) {
            putstr("\n");
        }
    }
}
```

```
function genArray(length) {
   var arr = [];
   for (var i = 0; i < length; ++i) {
      arr[i] = Math.floor(Math.random() * 101);
   }
   return arr;
}
```

Example 10-6 presents a program for testing out this new code for counting occurrences of grades.

Example 10-6. Counting occurrences of grades in a data set

```
function prArray(arr) {
   putstr(arr[0].toString() + ' ');
   for (var i = 1; i < arr.length; ++i) {
      putstr(arr[i].toString() + ' ');
      if (i % 10 == 0) {
         putstr("\n");
      }
   }
}


function genArray(length) {
   var arr = [];
   for (var i = 0; i < length; ++i) {
      arr[i] = Math.floor(Math.random() * 101);
   }
   return arr;
}

load("BSTtree.js");

var grades = genArray(100);
prArray(grades);
var gradedistro = new BST();
for (var i = 0; i < grades.length; ++i) {
   var g = grades[i];
   var grade = gradedistro.find(g);
   if (grade === null) {
      gradedistro.insert(g);
   }
   else {
      gradedistro.update(g);
   }
}
var cont = "y";

while (cont == "y") {
```

```
    putstr("\n\nEnter a grade: ");
    var g = parseInt(readline());
    var aGrade = gradedistro.find(g);
    if (aGrade === null) {
        print("No occurrences of " + g);
    }
    else {
        print("Occurrences of " + g + ": " + aGrade.count);
    }
    putstr("Look at another grade (y/n)? ");
    cont = readline();
}
```

Here is the output from one run of the program:

```
25 32 24 92 80 46 21 85 23 22 3
24 43 4 100 34 82 76 69 51 44
92 54 1 88 4 66 62 74 49 18
15 81 95 80 4 64 13 30 51 21
12 64 82 81 38 100 17 76 62 32
3 24 47 86 49 100 49 81 100 49
80 0 28 79 34 64 40 81 35 23
95 90 92 13 28 88 31 82 16 93
12 92 52 41 27 53 31 35 90 21
22 66 87 80 83 66 3 6 18

Enter a grade: 78
No occurrences of 78
Look at another grade (y/n)? y

Enter a grade: 65
No occurrences of 65
Look at another grade (y/n)? y

Enter a grade: 23
Occurrences of 23: 2
Look at another grade (y/n)? y

Enter a grade: 89
No occurrences of 89
Look at another grade (y/n)? y

Enter a grade: 100
Occurrences of 100: 4
Look at another grade (y/n)? n
```

Exercises

1. Add a function to the BST class that counts the number of nodes in a BST.

2. Add a function to the BST class that counts the number of edges in a BST.

3. Add a `max()` function to the BST class that finds the maximum value in a BST.

4. Add a `min()` function to the BST class that finds the minimum value in a BST.

5. Write a program that stores the words from a large text file in a BST and displays the number of times each word occurs in the text.

CHAPTER 11

Graphs and Graph Algorithms

The study of networks has become one of the great scientific hotbeds of this century, though mathematicians and others have been studying networks for many hundreds of years. Recent developments in computer technology (the Internet, for example) and in social theory (the social network, as popularized by the concept of "six degrees of separation"), not to mention social media, have put a spotlight on the study of networks.

In this chapter we'll look at how networks are modeled with graphs. We'll define what a graph is, how to represent graphs in JavaScript, and how to implement important graph algorithms. We'll also discuss the importance of choosing the correct data representation when working with graphs, since the efficiency of graph algorithms largely depends on the data structure used to represent a graph.

Graph Definitions

A graph consists of a set of *vertices* and a set of *edges*. Think of a map of a US state. Each town is connected with other towns via some type of road. A map is a type of graph where each town is a vertex, and a road that connects two towns is an edge. Edges are defined as a pair (v1, v2), where v1 and v2 are two vertices in a graph. A vertex can also have a weight, which is sometimes called a cost. A graph whose pairs are ordered is called a *directed graph*, or just a *digraph*. When pairs are ordered in a directed graph, an arrow is drawn from one pair to another pair. Directed graphs indicate the flow direction from vertex to vertex. A flowchart that indicates the direction of computations in a computer program is an example of a directed graph. A directed graph is shown in Figure 11-1.

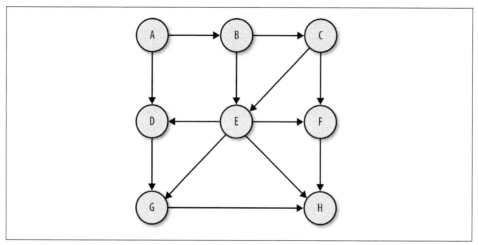

Figure 11-1. A digraph (directed graph)

If a graph is not ordered, it is called an *unordered graph*, or just a graph. An example of an unordered graph is shown in Figure 11-2.

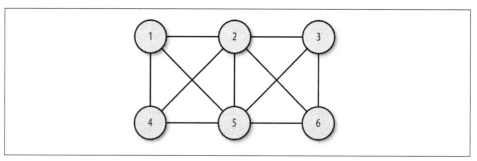

Figure 11-2. An unordered graph

A *path* is a sequence of vertices in a graph such that all vertices in the path are connected by edges. The length of a path is the number of edges from the first vertex in the path to the last vertex. A path can also consist of a vertex to itself, which is called a loop. Loops have a length of 0.

A *cycle* is a path with at least one edge whose first and last vertices are the same. A *simple cycle* is one with no repeated edges or vertices for both directed and undirected graphs. Paths that repeat other vertices besides the first and last vertices are called *general cycles*.

Two vertices are considered *strongly* connected if there is a path from the first vertex to the second vertex, and vice versa. If the graph is a directed graph, and all its vertices are strongly connected, then the directed graph is considered strongly connected.

Real-World Systems Modeled by Graphs

Graphs are used to model many different types of real-world systems. One example is traffic flow. The vertices represent street intersections, and the edges represent the streets. Weighted edges can be used to represent speed limits or the number of lanes. Modelers can use the system to determine the best routes and the streets most likely to suffer from traffic jams.

Any type of transportation system can be modeled using a graph. For example, an airline can model its flight system using a graph. Each airport is a vertex, and each flight from one vertex to another is an edge. A weighted edge can represent the cost of a flight from one airport to another, or perhaps the distance from one airport to another, depending upon what is being modeled.

Computer networks, including local area networks and much broader networks such as the Internet, are also frequently modeled with graphs. Another example of a real-word system that can be modeled by a graph is a consumer market, where vertices represent both institutions (vendors) and consumers.

The Graph Class

At first glance, a graph looks much like a tree or a binary tree, and you might be tempted to try to build a graph class like a tree, using nodes to represent each vertex. There are problems with using an object-based approach like that, however, because graphs can grow quite large. Representing a graph using just objects can quickly become inefficient, so we will look at a different scheme for representing both vertices and edges.

Representing Edges

The real information about a graph is stored in the edges, since the edges describe the structure of a graph. As we mentioned earlier, it is tempting to represent a graph as a binary tree, but doing so is a mistake. A binary tree has a mostly fixed representation, since a parent node can have only two child nodes, while a graph structure provides much more flexibility. There can be many edges linked to a single vertex or just one edge, for example.

The method we will use for representing the edges of a graph is called an *adjacency list*, or an *array of adjacency lists*. With this method, the edges are stored as a vertex-indexed array of lists (arrays) of the vertices adjacent to each vertex. Using this scheme, when we reference a vertex in a program, we can efficiently access the list of all the vertices it is connected to. For example, if the vertex 2 is connected to vertices 0, 1, 3, and 4, and is stored in array position 2, accessing this element gives us access to an array stored at array position 2 that consists of the vertices 0, 1, 3, and 4. This is the representation method we choose to use in this chapter and is shown in Figure 11-3.

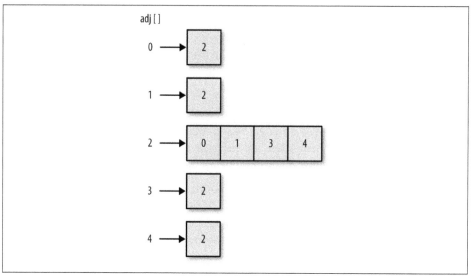

Figure 11-3. An adjacency list

Another method for representing the the edges of a graph is called an *adjacency matrix*. This is a two-dimensional array in which the elements of the array indicate whether an edge exists between two vertices.

Building a Graph

Once the decision is made on how to represent a graph in code, building a class to represent a graph is straightforward. Here is a first definition of a Graph class:

```
function Graph(v) {
    this.vertices = v;
    this.edges = 0;
    this.adj = [];
    for (var i = 0; i < this.vertices; ++i) {
        this.adj[i] = [];
    }
    this.addEdge = addEdge;
    this.showGraph = showGraph;
}
```

The class keeps track of how many edges are represented in a graph, as well as the number of vertices, by utilizing an array whose length is equal to the number of vertices in the graph. In each element of the array, the for loop adds a subarray to store all the adjacent vertices.

The addEdge() function is defined as:

```
function addEdge(v,w) {
    this.adj[v].push(w);
    this.adj[w].push(v);
    this.edges++;
}
```

When this function is called with two vertices, A and B, the function finds the adjacency list for vertex A and adds B to the list, then it finds the adjacency list for B and adds A to the list. Finally, the function increments the number of edges by 1.

The showGraph() function displays the graph by showing a list of all vertices and the vertices that are adjacent to them:

```
function showGraph() {
    for (var i = 0; i < this.vertices; ++i) {
        putstr(i + " -> ");
        for (var j = 0; j < this.vertices; ++j) {
            if (this.adj[i][j] != undefined)
                putstr(this.adj[i][j] + ' ');
        }
        print();
    }
}
```

Example 11-1 displays the complete definition for the Graph class.

Example 11-1. The Graph class

```
function Graph(v) {
    this.vertices = v;
    this.edges = 0;
    this.adj = [];
    for (var i = 0; i < this.vertices; ++i) {
        this.adj[i] = [];
    }
    this.addEdge = addEdge;
    this.showGraph = showGraph;
}


function addEdge(v,w) {
    this.adj[v].push(w);
    this.adj[w].push(v);
    this.edges++;
}

function showGraph() {
    for (var i = 0; i < this.vertices; ++i) {
        putstr(i + " -> ");
        for (var j = 0; j < this.vertices; ++j) {
```

```
            if (this.adj[i][j] != undefined)
                putstr(this.adj[i][j] + ' ');
        }
        print();
    }
}
```

Here is a test program that demonstrates how to use the Graph class:

```
load("Graph.js");
g = new Graph(5);
g.addEdge(0,1);
g.addEdge(0,2);
g.addEdge(1,3);
g.addEdge(2,4);
g.showGraph();
```

The output from this program is:

```
0 ->  1 2
1 ->  0 3
2 ->  0 4
3 ->  1
4 ->  2
```

The output shows that vertex 0 has edges to vertices 1 and 2; vertex 1 has edges to vertices 0 and 3; vertex 2 has edges to vertices 0 and 4; vertex 3 has an edge to vertex 1; and vertex 4 has an edge to vertex 2. Of course, there is some redundancy in this display, as an edge between 0 and 1, for example, is the same as an edge between 1 and 0. For just display purposes this is fine, but we will need to modify this output when we start exploring the paths found in a graph.

Searching a Graph

Determining which vertices can be reached from a specified vertex is a common activity performed on graphs. We might want to know which roads lead from one town to other towns on the map, or which flights can take us from one airport to other airports.

These operations are performed on a graph using a search algorithm. There are two fundamental searches we can perform on a graph: the *depth-first* search and the *breadth-first* search. In this section we examine both algorithms.

Depth-First Search

Depth-first search involves following a path from the beginning vertex until it reaches the last vertex, then backtracking and following the next path until it reaches the last vertex, and so on until there are no paths left. Here we are not "searching" for a particular item, but instead searching to see what paths we can follow in a graph. Figure 11-4 illustrates how depth-first search works.

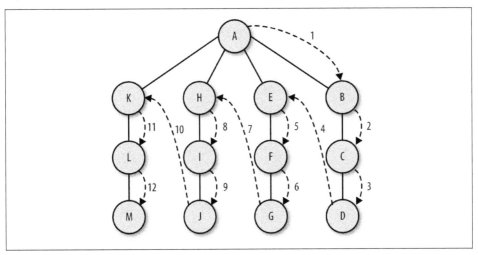

Figure 11-4. Depth-first search

The algorithm for performing a depth-first search is relatively simple—visit a vertex that has not already been visited, mark it as having been visited, then recursively visit the other unvisited vertices that are in the original vertex's adjacency list.

To make this algorithm work, we will need to add an array to our Graph class that stores visited vertices and initialize it to all false values. Here is a code fragment from the Graph class showing this new array and its initialization:

```
this.marked = [];
for (var i = 0; i < this.vertices; ++i) {
    this.marked[i] = false;
}
```

Now we can write the depth-first search function:

```
function dfs(v) {
    this.marked[v] = true;
    if (this.adj[v] !== undefined) {
        print("Visited vertex: " + v);
    }
    for (var i = 0; i < this.adj[v].length; i++) {
        var w = this.adj[v][i];
        if (!this.marked[w]) {
            this.dfs(w);
        }
    }
}
```

Notice that I've included a print() function so we can see the vertices as they're being visited. This function is, of course, not required for the dfs() function to work properly.

A program that demonstrates the depthFirst() function is shown in Example 11-2, after adding dfs() to the Graph class.

Example 11-2. Performing a depth-first search

```
// program to test dfs() function

load("Graph.js");
g = new Graph(5);
g.addEdge(0,1);
g.addEdge(0,2);
g.addEdge(1,3);
g.addEdge(2,4);
g.showGraph();
g.dfs(0);
```

The output from this program is:

```
0 ->  1 2
1 ->  0 3
2 ->  0 4
3 ->  1
4 ->  2
Visited vertex: 0
Visited vertex: 1
Visited vertex: 3
Visited vertex: 2
Visited vertex: 4
```

Breadth-First Search

A breadth-first search starts at a first vertex and tries to visit vertices as close to the first vertex as possible. In essence, this search moves through a graph layer by layer, first examining layers closer to the first vertex and then moving down to the layers farthest away from the starting vertex. Figure 11-5 demonstrates how breadth-first search works.

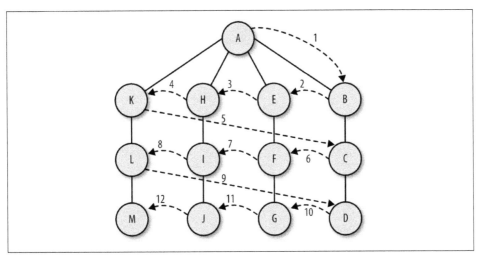

Figure 11-5. Breadth-first search

The algorithm for breadth-first search uses a queue abstraction instead of an array abstraction for storing visited vertices. The algorithm works as follows:

1. Find an unvisited vertex that is adjacent to the current vertex, add it to the list of visited vertices, and add it to the queue.
2. Take the next vertex, *v*, from the graph and add it to the list of visited vertices.
3. Add all unmarked vertices that are are adjacent to v and add them to the queue.

Here is the definition for the breadth-first search function:

```
function bfs(s) {
    var queue = [];
    this.marked[s] = true;
    queue.push(s); // add to back of queue
    while (queue.length > 0) {
        var v = queue.shift(); // remove from front of queue
        if (v !== undefined) {
            print("Visited vertex: " + v);
        }
        for (var i = 0; i < this.adj[v].length; i++) {
            var w = this.adj[v][i];
            if (!this.marked[w]) {
                this.marked[w] = true;
                queue.push(w);
            }
        }
    }
}
```

It's added to the Graph class with the addition of the following to the class:

```
        this.bfs = bfs;
```

A test program for the breadth-first search function is shown in Example 11-3.

Example 11-3. Performing a breadth-first search

```
load("Graph.js");
g = new Graph(5);
g.addEdge(0,1);
g.addEdge(0,2);
g.addEdge(1,3);
g.addEdge(2,4);
g.showGraph();
g.bfs(0);
```

The output from this program is:

```
0 ->  1 2
1 ->  0 3
2 ->  0 4
3 ->  1
4 ->  2
Visited vertex: 0
Visited vertex: 1
Visited vertex: 2
Visited vertex: 3
Visited vertex: 4
```

Finding the Shortest Path

One of the most common operations performed on graphs is finding the shortest path from one vertex to another. Consider the following example: for vacation, you are going to travel to 10 major-league cities to watch baseball games over a two-week period. You want to minimize the number of miles you have to drive to visit all 10 cities using a shortest-path algorithm. Another shortest-path problem involves creating a network of computers, where the cost could be the time to transmit data between two computers or the cost of establishing and maintaining the connection. A shortest-path algorithm can determine the most effective way to build the network.

Breadth-First Search Leads to Shortest Paths

When we perform a breadth-first search, we are automatically finding the shortest paths from one vertex to another connected vertex. For example, when we want to find the shortest path from vertex A to vertex D, we first look for any one-edge paths from A to D, then two-edge paths from A to D, and so on. This is exactly the way breadth-first search works, so we can easily modify the breadth-first search algorithm to find shortest paths.

Determining Paths

To find the shortest path, we need to modify the breadth-first search algorithm so that it records the paths that lead from one vertex to another vertex. This requires a few modifications to the Graph class.

First, we need an array that keeps track of edges from one vertex to the next. We'll name this array edgeTo. As we work through the breadth-first search function, every time we come across a vertex that is not marked, besides marking it, we will add an edge to that vertex from the vertex that we are exploring in the adjacency list. Here is the new bfs() function, along with the code you need to add the edgeTo array to the Graph class:

```
// add this to Graph class
this.edgeTo = [];

// bfs function
function bfs(s) {
    var queue = [];
    this.marked[s] = true;
    queue.push(s); // add to back of queue
    while (queue.length > 0) {
        var v = queue.shift(); // remove from front of queue
        if (v !== undefined) {
            print("Visited vertex: " + v);
        }
        for (var i = 0; i < this.adj[v].length; i++) {
            var w = this.adj[v][i];
            if (!this.marked[w]) {
                this.edgeTo[w] = v;
                this.marked[w] = true;
                queue.push(w);
            }
        }
    }
}
```

Now we need a function that can show us the paths that connect the different vertices of a graph. This function, pathTo(), creates a stack that stores all the vertices that have edges in common with a specified vertex. Here is the code for the function, along with a simple helper function:

```
function pathTo(source, v) {
    if (!this.hasPathTo(v)) {
        return undefined;
    }
    var path = [];
    for (var i = v; i != source; i = this.edgeTo[i]) {
        path.push(i);
    }
    path.push(source);
```

```
        return path;
    }

    function hasPathTo(v) {
        return this.marked[v];
    }
```

Lastly, we add a function that prints out the path:

```
function showPath(paths) {
    while (paths.length > 0) {
        if (paths.length > 1) {
            putstr(paths.pop() + '-');
        }
        else {
            putstr(paths.pop());
        }
    }
}
```

Be sure to add the appropriate declarations to the Graph() function:

```
this.pathTo = pathTo;
this.hasPathTo = hasPathTo;
this.showPath = showPath;
```

With this function, all we have to do is write some client code to show the shortest path from the source to a particular vertex. Example 11-4 shows a program that creates a graph and shows the shortest path for a specified vertex.

Example 11-4. Finding the shortest path for a vertex

```
load("Graph.js");
g = new Graph(5);
g.addEdge(0,1);
g.addEdge(0,2);
g.addEdge(1,3);
g.addEdge(2,4);
g.bfs(0);
var vertex = 4;
var source = 0;
var paths = g.pathTo(source,vertex);
g.showPath(paths);
```

The output from showPath() is:

```
0-2-4
```

which is the shortest path from the source vertex 0 to vertex 4.

Topological Sorting

Topological sorting puts the vertices of a directed graph into an order such that all the directed edges point from a vertex earlier in the order to a vertex later in the order. For example, Figure 11-6 shows a directed-graph model of a typical computer science curriculum.

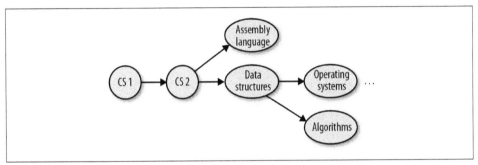

Figure 11-6. A directed graph model of a computer science curriculum

A topological sort of this graph would result in the following sequence:

1. CS 1
2. CS 2
3. Assembly language
4. Data structures
5. Operating systems
6. Algorithms

Courses 3 and 4 can be taken at the same time, as can courses 5 and 6.

This type of problem is called *precedence-constrained scheduling*, and every college student is familiar with it. You can't take English Composition II until you've taken English Composition I.

An Algorithm for Topological Sorting

The algorithm for topological sorting is similar to the algorithm for depth-first search. However, instead of immediately printing a vertex as it is visited, the algorithm visits all the adjacent vertices to the current vertex, and once that list is exhausted, we push the current vertex onto a stack.

Implementing the Topological Sorting Algorithm

The topological sort algorithm is broken up into two functions. The first function, topSort(), sets up the sorting process and calls a helper function, topSortHelper(), and then displays the sorted list of vertices.

The major work is done in the recursive function topSortHelper(). This function marks the current vertex as visited and then recursively visits each adjacent vertex in the current vertex's adjacency list, marking them as visited. Finally, the current vertex is pushed onto a stack.

Example 11-5 shows the code for the two functions.

Example 11-5. topSort() and topSortHelper()

```
function topSort() {
   var stack = [];
   var visited = [];
   for (var i = 0; i < this.vertices; i++) {
      visited[i] = false;
   }
   for (var i = 0; i < this.vertices; i++) {
      if (!visited[i]) {
         this.topSortHelper(i, visited, stack);
      }
   }
   for (var i = 0; i < stack.length; i++) {
      if (stack[i] != undefined && stack[i] != false) {
         print(this.vertexList[stack[i]]);
      }
   }
}

function topSortHelper(v, visited, stack) {
   visited[v] = true;
   for (var i = 0; i < this.adj[v]; i++) {
      w = this.adj[v][i];
      if (!visited[w]) {
         this.topSortHelper(visited[w], visited, stack);
      }
   }
   stack.push(v);
}
```

The Graph class has also been modified so that we can work with symbolic vertices and not just numbers. Inside the code, each vertex is still only numbered, but we add an array, vertexList, which associates each vertex with a symbol (for our example it's a course name).

To make sure the new definition of the class is clear, we present the full definition, including the functions for topological sorting, below. The definition of the function showGraph() has changed so that symbolic names are shown instead of just vertex numbers. Example 11-6 shows the code.

Example 11-6. The Graph class

```
function Graph(v) {
   this.vertices = v;
   this.vertexList = [];
   this.edges = 0;
   this.adj = [];
   for (var i = 0; i < this.vertices; ++i) {
      this.adj[i] = [];
   }
   this.addEdge = addEdge;
   this.showGraph = showGraph;
   this.dfs = dfs;
   this.marked = [];
   for (var i = 0; i < this.vertices; ++i) {
      this.marked[i] = false;
   }
   this.bfs = bfs;
   this.edgeTo = [];
   this.hasPathTo = hasPathTo;
   this.pathTo = pathTo;
   this.topSortHelper = topSortHelper;
   this.topSort = topSort;

}

function topSort() {
   var stack = [];
   var visited = [];
   for (var i = 0; i < this.vertices; i++) {
      visited[i] = false;
   }
   for (var i = 0; i < this.vertices; i++) {
      if (!visited[i]) {
         this.topSortHelper(i, visited, stack);
      }
   }
   for (var i = 0; i < stack.length; i++) {
      if (stack[i] !== undefined && stack[i] !== false) {
         print(this.vertexList[stack[i]]);
      }
   }
}

function topSortHelper(v, visited, stack) {
   visited[v] = true;
```

```
      for (var i = 0; i < this.adj[v]; i++) {
         var w = this.adj[v][i];
         if (!visited[w]) {
            this.topSortHelper(visited[w], visited, stack);
         }
      }
      stack.push(v);
   }

   function addEdge(v,w) {
      this.adj[v].push(w);
      this.adj[w].push(v);
      this.edges++;
   }

   // a new function to display symbolic names instead of numbers
   function showGraph() {
      for (var i = 0; i < this.vertices; ++i) {
         putstr(this.vertexList[i] + " -> ");
         for (var j = 0; j < this.vertices; ++j) {
            if (this.adj[i][j] !== undefined) {
               var w = this.adj[i][j];
               putstr(this.vertexList[w] + ' ');
            }
         }
         print();
      }
   }


   function dfs(v) {
      this.marked[v] = true;
      if (this.adj[v] !== undefined) {
         print("Visited vertex: " + v);
      }
      for (var i = 0; i < this.adj[v].length; i++) {
         var w = this.adj[v][w];
         if (!this.marked[w]) {
            this.dfs(w);
         }
      }
   }

   function bfs(s) {
      var queue = [];
      this.marked[s] = true;
      queue.push(s); // add to back of queue
      while (queue.length > 0) {
         var v = queue.shift(); // remove from front of queue
         if (v !== undefined) {
            console.log("Visited vertex: " + v);
         }
```

```
        for (var i = 0; i < this.adj[v].length; i++) {
            var w = this.adj[v][i];
            if (!this.marked[w]) {
                this.edgeTo[w] = v;
                this.marked[w] = true;
                queue.push(w);
            }
        }
    }
}

function hasPathTo(v) {
    return this.marked[v];
}

function pathTo(source, v) {
    if (!this.hasPathTo(v)) {
        return undefined;
    }
    var path = [];
    for (var i = v; i != source; i = this.edgeTo[i]) {
        path.push(i);
    }
    path.push(source);
    return path;
}
```

A program that tests our implementation of topological sorting is shown in Example 11-7.

Example 11-7. Topological sorting

```
load("GraphTopo.js");
g = new Graph(6);
g.addEdge(1,2);
g.addEdge(2,5);
g.addEdge(1,3);
g.addEdge(1,4);
g.addEdge(0,1);
g.vertexList = ["CS1", "CS2", "Data Structures",
                "Assembly Language", "Operating Systems",
                "Algorithms"];
g.showGraph();
print();
g.topSort();
```

The output from this program is:

```
    CS1 -> CS2
    CS2 -> Data Structures Assembly Language Operating Systems CS1
    Data Structures -> CS2 Algorithms
    Assembly Language -> CS2
```

```
Operating Systems -> CS2
Algorithms -> Data Structures

CS1
CS2
Data Structures
Assembly Language
Operating Systems
Algorithms
```

Exercises

1. Write a program that determines which type of graph search is faster—breadth-first or depth-first. Test your program with graphs of many different sizes.

2. Write a program that stores a graph in a file.

3. Write a program that reads a graph from a file.

4. Build a graph that models the map of the area where you live. Determine the shortest path from a starting vertex to the last vertex.

5. Perform a depth-first search and a breadth-first search of the graph created in example 4.

CHAPTER 12

Sorting Algorithms

Two of the most common operations performed on data stored in a computer are sorting and searching. This has been true since the beginning of the computer industry, so this means that sorting and searching are two of the most studied operations in computer science. Many of the data structures discussed in this book are designed primarily to make sorting and/or searching the data stored in the data structure easier and more efficient.

This chapter will introduce you to some of the basic and advanced algorithms for sorting data. These algorithms depend only on the array as the means of storing data. In this chapter we'll also look at ways of timing our programs to determine which algorithm is most efficient.

An Array Test Bed

We start this chapter by developing an array test bed to use in support of our study of basic sorting algorithms. We'll build a class for array data and functions that encapsulates some of the normal array operations: inserting new data, displaying array data, and calling the different sorting algorithms. Included in the class is a swap() function we will use to exchange elements in the array.

Example 12-1 shows the code for this class.

Example 12-1. Array test bed class

```
function CArray(numElements) {
   this.dataStore = [];
   this.pos = 0;
   this.numElements = numElements;
   this.insert = insert;
   this.toString = toString;
   this.clear = clear;
   this.setData = setData;
   this.swap = swap;

   for (var i = 0; i < numElements; ++i) {
      this.dataStore[i] = i;
   }
}

function setData() {
   for (var i = 0; i < this.numElements; ++i) {
      this.dataStore[i] = Math.floor(Math.random() *
                          (this.numElements+1));
   }
}

function clear() {
   for (var i = 0; i < this.dataStore.length; ++i) {
      this.dataStore[i] = 0;
   }
}

function insert(element) {
   this.dataStore[this.pos++] = element;
}

function toString() {
   var retstr = "";
   for (var i = 0; i < this.dataStore.length; ++i) {
      retstr += this.dataStore[i] + " ";
      if (i > 0 && i % 10 == 0) {
         retstr += "\n";
      }
   }
   return retstr;
}

function swap(arr, index1, index2) {
   var temp = arr[index1];
   arr[index1] = arr[index2];
   arr[index2] = temp;
}
```

Here is a simple program that uses the `CArray` class (the class is named `CArray` because JavaScript already has an `Array` class):

Example 12-2. Using the test bed class

```
var numElements = 100;
var myNums = new CArray(numElements);
myNums.setData();
print(myNums.toString());
```

The output from this program is, though it will be different when you run it because of the use of the random number generator in `setData()`:

```
76 69 64 4 64 73 47 34 65 93 32
59 4 92 84 55 30 52 64 38 74
40 68 71 25 84 5 57 7 6 40
45 69 34 73 87 63 15 96 91 96
88 24 58 78 18 97 22 48 6 45
68 65 40 50 31 80 7 39 72 84
72 22 66 84 14 58 11 42 7 72
87 39 79 18 18 9 84 18 45 50
43 90 87 62 65 97 97 21 96 39
7 79 68 35 39 89 43 86 5
```

Generating Random Data

The `setData()` function generates random numbers to store in the array. The `random()` function, which is part of the `Math` class, generates random numbers in a range from 0 to 1, exclusive. In other words, no random number generated by the function will equal 0, and no random number will equal 1. These random numbers are not very useful, so we scale the numbers by multiplying the random number by the number of elements we want plus 1, and then use the `floor()` function from the `Math` class to finalize the number. As you can see from the preceding output, this formula succeeds in generating a set of random numbers between 1 and 100.

For more information on how JavaScript generates random numbers, see the Mozilla page, Using the Math.random() function (*http://mzl.la/1nwbDYh*), for random number generation.

Basic Sorting Algorithms

The fundamental concept of the basic sorting algorithms covered next is that there is a list of data that needs to be rearranged into sorted order. The technique used in these algorithms to rearrange data in a list is a set of nested `for` loops. The outer loop moves through the list item by item, while the inner loop is used to compare elements. These algorithms very closely simulate how humans sort data in real life, such as how a card player sorts cards when dealt a hand or how a teacher sorts papers in alphabetical or grade order.

Bubble Sort

The first sorting algorithm we will examine is the *bubble sort*. The bubble sort is one of the slowest sorting algorithms, but it is also one of the easiest sorts to implement.

The bubble sort gets its name because when data are sorted using the algorithm, values float like a bubble from one end of the array to the other. Assuming you are sorting a set of numbers into ascending order, larger values float to the right of the array and lower values float to the left. This behavior is the result of the algorithm moving through the array many times, comparing adjacent values, and swapping them if the value to the left is greater than the value to the right.

Here is a simple example of the bubble sort. We start with the following list:

E A D B H

The first pass of the sort yields the following list:

A E D B H

The first and second elements are swapped. The next pass of the sort leads to:

A D E B H

The second and third elements are swapped. The next pass leads to the following order:

A D B E H

as the third and fourth elements are swapped. And finally, the second and third elements are swapped again, leading to the final order:

A B D E H

Figure 12-1 illustrates how the bubble sort works with a larger data set of numbers. In the figure, we examine two particular values inserted into the array: 2 and 72. Each number is circled. You can watch how 72 moves from the beginning of the array to the middle of the array, and you can watch how 2 moves from just past the middle of the array to the beginning of the array.

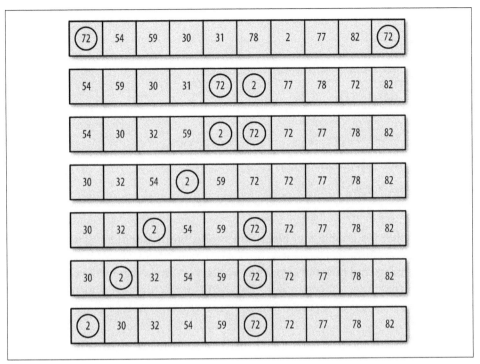

Figure 12-1. Bubble sort in action

Example 12-3 shows the code for the bubble sort:

Example 12-3. The bubbleSort() function

```
function bubbleSort() {
   var numElements = this.dataStore.length;
   var temp;
   for (var outer = numElements; outer >= 2; --outer) {
      for (var inner = 0; inner <= outer-1; ++inner) {
         if (this.dataStore[inner] > this.dataStore[inner+1]) {
            swap(this.dataStore, inner, inner+1);
         }
      }
   }
}
```

Be sure to add a call to this function to the `CArray` constructor. Example 12-4 is a short program that sorts 10 numbers using the `bubbleSort()` function.

Example 12-4. Sorting 10 numbers with bubbleSort()

```
load("carray.js");
var numElements = 10;
var mynums = new CArray(numElements);
mynums.setData();
print(mynums.toString());
mynums.bubbleSort();
print();
print(mynums.toString());
```

The output from this program is:

```
9 2 2 3 3 2 9 8 9 3

2 2 2 3 3 3 8 9 9 9
```

We can see that the bubble sort algorithm works, but it would be nice to view the intermediate results of the algorithm, since a record of the sorting process is useful in helping us understand how the algorithm works. We can do that by the careful place-ment of the toString() function into the bubbleSort() function, which will display the current state of the array as the function proceeds (shown in Example 12-5).

Example 12-5. Adding a call to the toString() *function to* bubbleSort()

```
function bubbleSort() {
   var numElements = this.dataStore.length;
   var temp;
   for (var outer = numElements; outer >= 2; --outer) {
      for (var inner = 0; inner <= outer-1; ++inner) {
         if (this.dataStore[inner] > this.dataStore[inner+1]) {
            swap(this.dataStore, inner, inner+1);
         }
      }
      print(this.toString());
   }
}
```

When we run the program in Example 12-4 with the modified bubbleSort(), we get the following output:

```
7 0 9 10 8 0 3 3 5 7
0 7 9 8 0 3 3 5 7 10
0 7 8 0 3 3 5 7 9 10
0 7 0 3 3 5 7 8 9 10
0 0 3 3 5 7 7 8 9 10
0 0 3 3 5 7 7 8 9 10
0 0 3 3 5 7 7 8 9 10
0 0 3 3 5 7 7 8 9 10
0 0 3 3 5 7 7 8 9 10
0 0 3 3 5 7 7 8 9 10
```

```
0 0 3 3 5 7 7 8 9 10
```

With this output, you can more easily see how the lower values work their way to the beginning of the array and how the higher values work their way to the end of the array.

Selection Sort

The next sorting algorithm we examine is the *selection sort*. This sort works by starting at the beginning of the array and comparing the first element with the remaining elements. After examining all the elements, the smallest element is placed in the first position of the array, and the algorithm moves to the second position. This process continues until the algorithm arrives at the next to last position in the array, at which point all the data is sorted.

Nested loops are used in the selection sort algorithm. The outer loop moves from the first element in the array to the next to last element; the inner loop moves from the second array element to the last element, looking for values that are smaller than the element currently being pointed to by the outer loop. After each iteration of the inner loop, the smallest value in the array is assigned its proper place in the array. Figure 12-2 illustrates how the selection sort algorithm works.

Here is a simple example of how selection sort works on a list of five items. The original list is:

E A D H B

The first pass looks for the minimal value and swaps it with the value at the front of the list:

A E D H B

The next pass finds the minimal value after the first element (which is now in place) and swaps it:

A B D H E

The D is in place so the next step swaps the E and the H, leading to the list being in order:

A B D E H

Figure 12-2 shows how selection sort works on a larger data set of numbers.

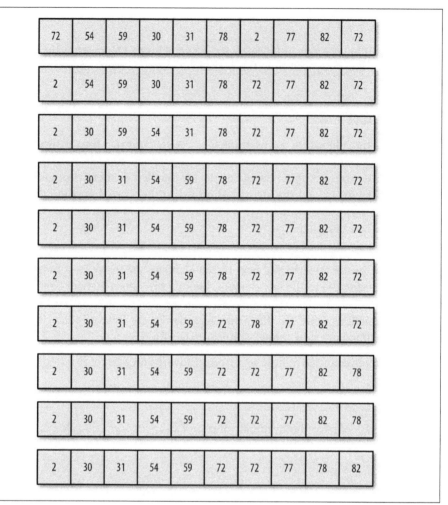

Figure 12-2. The selection sort algorithm

Example 12-6 shows the code for the selectionSort() function.

Example 12-6. The selectionSort() function

```
function selectionSort() {
  var min, temp;
  for (var outer = 0; outer <= this.dataStore.length-2; ++outer) {
    min = outer;
    for (var inner = outer + 1;
         inner <= this.dataStore.length-1; ++inner) {
      if (this.dataStore[inner] < this.dataStore[min]) {
        min = inner;
```

```
        }
    }
    swap(this.dataStore, outer, min);
    print(this.toString());
  }
}
```

Replace the bubbleSort() call in Example 12-4 with a call to the new selection Sort(). Below is the output from one run of our program using the selection Sort() function.

```
6 10 4 9 7 9 1 7 5 0
0 10 4 9 7 9 1 7 5 6
0 1 4 9 7 9 10 7 5 6
0 1 4 9 7 9 10 7 5 6
0 1 4 5 7 9 10 7 9 6
0 1 4 5 6 9 10 7 9 7
0 1 4 5 6 7 10 9 9 7
0 1 4 5 6 7 7 9 9 10
0 1 4 5 6 7 7 9 9 10
0 1 4 5 6 7 7 9 9 10

0 1 4 5 6 7 7 9 9 10
```

Insertion Sort

The *insertion sort* is analogous to the way humans sort data numerically or alphabeti-cally. Let's say I have asked each student in a class to turn in an index card with his or her name, student ID, and a short biographical sketch. The students return the cards in random order, but I want them alphabetized so I can compare them to my class roster easily.

I take the cards back to my office, clear off my desk, and pick the first card. The last name on the card is Smith. I place it at the top left corner of the desk and pick the second card. The last name on the card is Brown. I move Smith over to the right and put Brown in Smith's place. The next card is Williams. It can be inserted at the far right of the desk without have to shift any of the other cards. The next card is Acklin. It has to go at the beginning of the list, so each of the other cards must be shifted one position to the right to make room for Acklin's card. This is how the insertion sort works.

The insertion sort has two loops. The outer loop moves element by element through the array, while the inner loop compares the element chosen in the outer loop to the element next to it in the array. If the element selected by the outer loop is less than the element selected by the inner loop, array elements are shifted over to the right to make room for the inner-loop element, just as described in the previous name card example.

Example 12-7 shows the code for the insertion sort. Be sure to add it to the CArray object.

Example 12-7. The `insertionSort()` function

```
function insertionSort() {
    var temp, inner;
    for (var outer = 1; outer <= this.dataStore.length-1; ++outer) {
        temp = this.dataStore[outer];
        inner = outer;
        while (inner > 0 && (this.dataStore[inner-1] >= temp)) {
            this.dataStore[inner] = this.dataStore[inner-1];
            --inner;
        }
        this.dataStore[inner] = temp;
        print(this.toString());
    }
}
```

Now let's look at how the insertion sort works by running Example 12-4 using the new `insertionSort()`:

```
4 3 3 5 2 5 1 10 10 1
3 4 3 5 2 5 1 10 10 1
3 3 4 5 2 5 1 10 10 1
3 3 4 5 2 5 1 10 10 1
2 3 3 4 5 5 1 10 10 1
2 3 3 4 5 5 1 10 10 1
1 2 3 3 4 5 5 10 10 1
1 2 3 3 4 5 5 10 10 1
1 2 3 3 4 5 5 10 10 1
1 1 2 3 3 4 5 5 10 10

1 1 2 3 3 4 5 5 10 10
```

This output clearly shows that the insertion sort works not by making data exchanges, but by moving larger array elements to the right to make room for the smaller elements on the left side of the array.

Timing Comparisons of the Basic Sorting Algorithms

These three sorting algorithms are very similar in complexity, and theoretically, they should perform similarly. To determine the differences in performance among these three algorithms, we can use an informal timing system to compare how long it takes them to sort data sets. Being able to time these algorithms is important because, while you won't see much of a difference in times of the sorting algorithms when you're sorting 100 elements or even 1,000 elements, there can be a huge difference in the times these algorithms take to sort millions of elements.

The timing system we will use in this section is based on retrieving the system time using the JavaScript Date object's getTime() function. Here is how the function works:

```
var start = new Date().getTime();
```

The getTime() function returns the system time in milliseconds. The following code fragment:

```
var start = new Date().getTime();
print(start);
```

results in the following output:

135154872720

To record the time it takes code to execute, we start the timer, run the code, and then stop the timer when the code is finished running. The time it takes to sort data is the difference between the recorded stopping time and the recorded starting time. Example 12-8 shows an example of timing a for loop that displays the numbers 1 through 100.

Example 12-8. Timing a for loop

```
var start = new Date().getTime();
for (var i = 1; i < 100; ++i) {
    print(i);
}
var stop = new Date().getTime();
var elapsed = stop - start;
print("The elapsed time was: " + elapsed +
      " milliseconds.");
```

The output, not including the starting and stopping time values, from the program is:

The elapsed time was: 91 milliseconds.

Now that we have a tool for measuring the efficiency of these sorting algorithms, let's run some tests to compare them.

For our comparison of the three basic sorting algorithms, we will time the three algorithms sorting arrays with data set sizes of 100, 1,000, and 10,000. We expect not to see much difference among the algorithms for data set sizes of 100 and 1,000, but we do expect there to be some difference when using a data set size of 10,000.

Let's start with an array of 100 randomly chosen integers. We also add a function for creating a new data set for each algorithm, and remove the print(this.toString()) from each of the sorting algorithms, to clean up the output. Example 12-9 shows the code for this new function.

Example 12-9. Timing the sorting functions with 100 array elements

```
load("carray3.js");
var numElements = 100;
var nums = new CArray(numElements);
nums.setData();
var start = new Date().getTime();
nums.bubbleSort();
var stop = new Date().getTime();
var elapsed = stop - start;
print("Elapsed time for the bubble sort on " +
      numElements + " elements is: " + elapsed + " milliseconds.");

nums.setData();
start = new Date().getTime();
nums.selectionSort();
stop = new Date().getTime();
elapsed = stop - start;
print("Elapsed time for the selection sort on " +
      numElements + " elements is: " +  elapsed + " milliseconds.");

nums.setData();
start = new Date().getTime();
nums.insertionSort();
stop = new Date().getTime();
elapsed = stop - start;
print("Elapsed time for the insertion sort on " +
      numElements + " elements is: " + elapsed + " milliseconds.");
```

Here are the results (note that I ran these tests on an Intel Core i5 2450M Processor 2.5GHz processor with 4 GB DIMM):

```
Elapsed time for the bubble sort on 100 elements is: 0 milliseconds.
Elapsed time for the selection sort on 100 elements is: 1 milliseconds.
Elapsed time for the insertion sort on 100 elements is: 0 milliseconds.
```

Clearly, there is not any significant difference among the three algorithms.

For the next test, we change the numElements variable to 1,000. Here are the results:

```
Elapsed time for the bubble sort on 1000 elements is: 17 milliseconds.
Elapsed time for the selection sort on 1000 elements is: 3 milliseconds.
Elapsed time for the insertion sort on 1000 elements is: 2 milliseconds.
```

For 1,000 numbers, the selection sort and the insertion sort are several times faster than the bubble sort.

Finally, we test the algorithms with 10,000 numbers:

```
Elapsed time for the bubble sort on 10000 elements is: 830 milliseconds.
Elapsed time for the selection sort on 10000 elements is: 85 milliseconds.
Elapsed time for the insertion sort on 10000 elements is: 65 milliseconds.
```

The results for 10,000 numbers are consistent with the results for 1,000 numbers. Selection sort and insertion sort are significantly faster than the bubble sort, and the insertion sort is the fastest of the three sorting algorithms. Keep in mind, however, that these tests must be run several times in a variety of environments for the results to be considered statistically valid.

Advanced Sorting Algorithms

In this section we will cover more advanced algorithms for sorting data. These sorting algorithms are generally considered the most efficient for large data sets, where data sets can have millions of elements rather than just hundreds or even thousands. The algorithms we study in this chapter include Quicksort, Shellsort, Mergesort, and Heapsort. We discuss each algorithm's implementation and then compare their efficiency by running timing tests.

The Shellsort Algorithm

The first advanced sorting algorithm we'll examine is the Shellsort algorithm. Shellsort is named after its inventor, Donald Shell. This algorithm is based on the insertion sort but is a big improvement over that basic sorting algorithm. Shellsort's key concept is that it compares distant elements first, rather than adjacent elements, as is done in the insertion sort. Elements that are far out of place can be put into place more efficiently using this scheme than by simply comparing neighboring elements. As the algorithm loops through the data set, the distance between each element decreases until, when at the end of the data set, the algorithm is comparing elements that are adjacent.

Shellsort works by defining a gap sequence that indicates how far apart compared elements are when starting the sorting process. The gap sequence can be defined dynamically, but for most practical applications, you can predefine the gap sequence the algorithm will use. There are several published gap sequences that produce different results. We are going to use the sequence defined by Marcin Ciura in his paper on best increments for average case of Shellsort ("Best Increments for the Average Case of Shell Sort" (*http://bit.ly/1b04YFv*), 2001). The gap sequence is: 701, 301, 132, 57, 23, 10, 4, 1. However, before we write code for the average case, we are going to examine how the algorithm works with a small data set.

Figure 12-3 demonstrates how the gap sequence works with the Shellsort algorithm.

Let's start with a look at the code for the Shellsort algorithm:

```
function shellsort() {
    for (var g = 0; g < this.gaps.length; ++g) {
        for (var i = this.gaps[g]; i < this.dataStore.length; ++i) {
            var temp = this.dataStore[i];
            for (var j = i; j >= this.gaps[g] &&
```

```
                        this.dataStore[j-this.gaps[g]] > temp;
            j -= this.gaps[g]) {
            this.dataStore[j] = this.dataStore[j - this.gaps[g]];
            print(this.toString());
        }
        this.dataStore[j] = temp;
    }
    print(this.toString());
    }
}
```

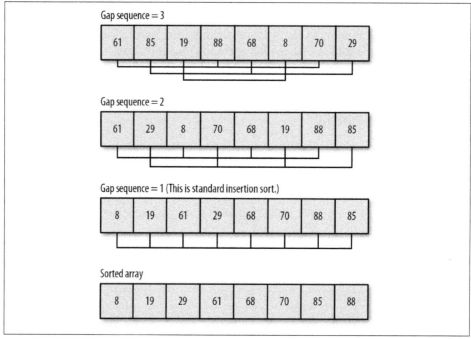

Figure 12-3. The Shellsort algorithm with an initial gap sequence of 3

For this program to work with our CArray class test bed, we need to add a definition of the gap sequence to the class definition. Add the following code into the constructor function for CArray:

```
this.gaps = [5,3,1];
```

And add this function to the object:

```
function setGaps(arr) {
    this.gaps = arr;
}
```

Finally, add a reference to the shellsort() function to the CArray class constructor as well as the shellsort() code itself.

The outer loop controls the movement within the gap sequence. In other words, for the first pass through the data set, the algorithm is going to examine elements that are five elements away from each other. The next pass will examine elements that are three elements away from each other. The last pass performs a standard insertion sort on element that are one place away, which means they are adjacent. By the time this last pass begins, many of the elements will already be in place, and the algorithm won't have to exchange many elements. This is where the algorithm gains efficiency over insertion sort. Figure 12-3 illustrates how the Shellsort algorithm works on a data set of 10 random numbers with a gap sequence of 5, 3, 1.

Now let's put the algorithm to work on a real example. We add a print() statement to shellsort() so that we can follow the progress of the algorithm while it sorts the data set. Each gap pass is noted, followed by the order of the data set after sorting with that particular gap. The program is shown in Example 12-10.

Example 12-10. Running shellsort() on a small data set

```
load("carray4.js")
var nums = new CArray(10);
nums.setData();
print("Before Shellsort: \n");
print(nums.toString());
print("\nDuring Shellsort: \n");
nums.shellsort();
print("\nAfter Shellsort: \n");
print(nums.toString());
```

The output from this program is:

```
Before Shellsort:

4 4 2 9 4 2 6 1 1 1

During Shellsort:

2 4 1 1 1 4 6 2 9 4
1 1 1 2 2 4 4 4 9 6
1 1 1 2 2 4 4 4 6 9

After Shellsort:

1 1 1 2 2 4 4 4 6 9
```

To understand how Shellsort works, compare the initial state of the array with its state after the gap sequence of 5 was sorted. The first element of the initial array, 4, was swapped with the fifth element after it, 1, because 1 < 4.

Now compare the gap 5 line with the gap 3 line. The 2 in the gap 5 line is swapped with the 1 because 1 < 2 and 1 is the third element after the 2. By simply counting the current gap sequence number down from the current element in the loop, and comparing the two numbers, you can trace any run of the Shellsort algorithm.

Having now seen some details of how the Shellsort algorithm works, let's use a larger gap sequence and run it with a larger data set (100 elements). Comment out the print() in the shellsort() method for a cleaner output Here is the output:

Before Shellsort:

```
100 96 80 59 74 55 92 24 93 73 71
42 55 2 56 46 50 20 20 95 19
94 21 77 9 92 22 41 64 11 67
70 23 12 98 46 58 73 92 3 23
7 39 46 22 70 36 72 43 85 26
96 78 2 62 0 29 82 48 88 88
50 10 17 7 55 54 42 89 56 89
41 74 75 29 80 71 10 67 54 32
72 33 30 81 86 90 79 4 30 84
31 29 42 10 78 68 29 49 17
```

After Shellsort:

```
0 2 2 3 4 7 7 9 10 10 10
11 12 17 17 19 20 20 21 22 22
23 23 24 26 29 29 29 29 30 30
31 32 33 36 39 41 41 42 42 42
43 46 46 46 48 49 50 50 54 54
55 55 55 56 56 58 59 62 64 67
67 68 70 70 71 71 72 72 73 73
74 74 75 77 78 78 79 80 80 81
82 84 85 86 88 88 89 89 90 92
92 92 93 94 95 96 96 98 100
```

We will revisit the shellsort() algorithm again when we compare it to other advanced sorting algorithms later in the chapter.

Computing a dynamic gap sequence

Robert Sedgewick, coauthor of *Algorithms, 4E* (Addison-Wesley), defines a shell sort() function that uses a formula to dynamically compute the gap sequence to use with Shellsort. Sedgewick's algorithm determines the initial gap value using the following code fragment:

```
var N = this.dataStore.length;
var h = 1;
while (h < N/3) {
    h = 3 * h + 1;
}
```

Once the gap value is determined, the function works like our previous shellsort() function, except the last statement before going back into the outer loop computes a new gap value:

```
h = (h-1)/3;
```

The complete, newly defined function is named `shellsort2()`, and is added to CArray:

```
function shellsort2() {
    var N = this.dataStore.length;
    var h = 1;
    while (h < N/3) {
        h = 3 * h + 1;
    }
    while (h >= 1) {
        for (var i = h; i < N; i++) {
            for (var j = i; j >= h && this.dataStore[j] < this.dataStore[j-h];
                j -= h) {
                swap(this.dataStore, j, j-h);
            }
        }
        h = (h-1)/3;
    }
}
```

Example 12-11 provides a program to test `shellsort2()`.

Example 12-11. shellsort() with a dynamically computed gap sequence

```
load("carray4.js")
var nums = new CArray(100);
nums.setData();
print("Before shellsort2: \n");
print(nums.toString());
nums.shellsort2();
print("\nAfter shellsort2: \n");
print(nums.toString());
```

The output from this program is:

```
Before shellsort2:

5 0 89 59 8 38 75 3 51 49 87
55 57 55 44 82 35 60 2 73 0
87 21 69 19 59 91 38 16 74 36
5 48 10 69 51 3 6 63 67 59
10 42 57 66 44 60 79 44 53 56
87 85 2 9 86 90 71 77 54 7
35 82 68 32 90 64 85 13 48 9
87 97 54 11 1 28 33 42 17 23
11 48 0 12 8 2 97 88 65 28
94 30 87 77 74 73 21 71 0

After shellsort2:
```

```
0 0 0 0 1 2 2 2 3 3 5
5 6 7 8 8 9 9 10 10 11
11 12 13 16 17 19 21 21 23 28
28 30 32 33 35 35 36 38 38 42
42 44 44 44 48 48 48 49 51 51
53 54 54 55 55 56 57 57 59 59
59 60 60 63 64 65 66 67 68 69
69 71 71 73 73 74 74 75 77 77
79 82 82 85 85 86 87 87 87 87
87 88 89 90 90 91 94 97 97
```

Before we leave the Shellsort algorithm, we need to compare the efficiency of our two shellsort() functions. First, to ensure that the test data store is clean before each test, we'll add a new method, clear(), to the CArray object:

```
function clear() {
    this.dataStore.length = 0;
}
```

A program that compares running times of the two functions is shown in Example 12-12. Both algorithms use Ciura's sequence for the gap sequence.

Example 12-12. Comparing shellsort() algorithms

```
load("carray4.js");
var nums = new CArray(10000);
nums.setData();
var start = new Date().getTime();
nums.shellsort();
var stop = new Date().getTime();
var elapsed = stop - start;
print("Shellsort with hard-coded gap sequence: " + elapsed + " ms.");
nums.clear();
nums.setData();
start = new Date().getTime();
nums.shellsort1();
stop = new Date().getTime();
print("Shellsort with dynamic gap sequence: " + elapsed + " ms.");
```

The results from this program are:

```
Shellsort with hard-coded gap sequence: 18 ms.
Shellsort with dynamic gap sequence: 18 ms.
```

Both algorithms sorted the data in the same amount of time. Here is the output from running the program with 100,000 data elements:

```
Shellsort with hard-coded gap sequence: 1578 ms.
Shellsort with dynamic gap sequence: 1578 ms.
```

Clearly, both of these algorithms sort data with the same efficiency, so you can use either of them with confidence.

The Mergesort Algorithm

The Mergesort algorithm is so named because it works by merging sorted sublists together to form a larger, completely sorted list. In theory, this algorithm should be easy to implement. We need two sorted subarrays and a third array into which we merge the two subarrays by comparing data elements and inserting the smallest element value. In practice, however, Mergesort has some problems because if we are trying to sort a very large data set using the algorithm, the amount of space we need to store the two merged subarrays can be quite large. Since space is not such an issue in these days of inexpensive memory, it is worth implementing Mergesort to see how it compares in efficiency to other sorting algorithms.

Bottom-up Mergesort

The nonrecursive, or iterative, version of Mergesort is referred to as a bottom-up process. The algorithm begins by breaking down the data set being sorted into a set of one-element arrays. Then these arrays are slowly merged by creating a set of left and right subarrays, each holding the partially sorted data until all that is left is one array with the data perfectly sorted.

Top-down Mergesort

It is customary to implement Mergesort as a recursive algorithm. The basic idea is that the array is split into two pieces, left and right. Each piece is then recursively split into its own left and right pieces, until the base case is reached, which is an array with a single element. Then the left and right pieces are merged into sorted order, on back up through the recursive calls until the outermost left and right partitions are merged, leaving the list in sorted order.

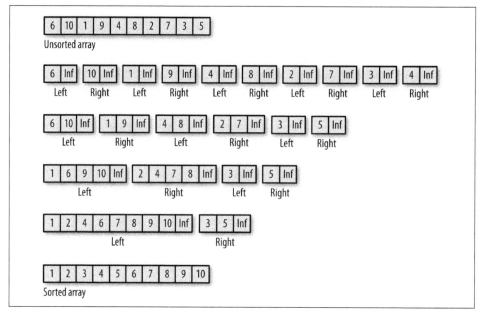

Figure 12-4. The bottom-up Mergesort algorithm

Before we show you the JavaScript code for Mergesort, here is the output from a Java-Script program that uses recursive Mergesort to sort an array of 10 integers:

```
6,10,1,9,4,8,2,7,3,5

left array -  6,10,1,9,4
left array -  6,10
left array -  6
right array - 10
merge arrays - 6,10
right array -  1,9,4
left array  -  1
right array - 9,4
left array - 9
right array - 4
merge arrays 4,9
merge arrays - 1,4,9
merge arrays - 1,4,6,9,10
(left array sorted)

right array -  8,2,7,3,5
left array -  8,2
left array - 8
right array - 2
merge arrays - 2,8
right array - 7,3,5
left array - 7
```

```
right array - 3,5
left array - 3
right array - 5
merge arrays - 3,5
merge arrays - 7,3,5
merge arrays - 2,3,5,7,8
(right array sorted)

merge arrays - 1,2,3,4,5,6,7,8,9,10

1,2,3,4,5,6,7,8,9,10
```

Now that we have seen how the recursive Mergesort works, Example 12-13 presents the code that created the preceding output.

Example 12-13. A recursive Mergesort JavaScript implementation

```javascript
function merge(left,right){
    var result = [];
    var leftLen = left.length;
    var rightLen = right.length;
    while (leftLen > 0 || rightLen > 0){
        if (leftLen > 0 && rightLen > 0){
        // Both left and right are still populated
            if (left[0] < right[0]){
                result.push(left.shift());
                leftLen -= 1;
            }
            else if (right[0] <= left[0]){
                result.push(right.shift());
                rightLen -= 1;
            }
        }
        // Only left array contains elements
        else if (leftLen > 0){
            result.push(left.shift());
            leftLen -= 1;
        }
        // Only right array contains elements
        else if (rightLen > 0){
            result.push(right.shift());
            rightLen -= 1;
        }
    }
    return result;
}

function mergeSort(array){
    var length = array.length;
    if (length <= 1){
      return array;
    }
```

```
            var q = Math.floor(length/2);
            var left = mergeSort(array.slice(0,q));
            var right = mergeSort(array.slice(q));
            return merge(left, right);
    }

var nums = [6,10,1,9,4,8,2,7,3,5];
print(nums);
print();
nums = mergeSort(nums);
print();
print(nums);
```

The key feature of the mergeSort() function is the recursive partitioning of the original list into successively smaller subarrays, until each consists of a single element. By controlling the size of the subarrays, the sort process is relatively efficient, since it doesn't take much time to sort a small array. This makes merging efficient also, since it is much easier to merge data into sorted order when the unmerged data is already sorted.

Our next step with Mergesort is to add it to the CArray class. Example 12-14 shows the CArray class with the mergeSort() and mergeArrays() functions added to its definition.

Example 12-14. Mergesort added to the CArray class

```
function CArray(numElements) {
  this.gaps = [5,3,1];
  this.dataStore = [];
  this.pos = 0;
  this.numElements = numElements;
  this.insert = insert;
  this.toString = toString;
  this.clear = clear;
  this.setData = setData;
  this.swap = swap;
  for (var i = 0; i < numElements; ++i) {
    this.dataStore[i] = i;
  this.bubbleSort = bubbleSort;
  this.selectionSort = selectionSort;
  this.insertionSort = insertionSort;
  this.shellSort = shellSort;
  this.shellSort2 = shellSort2;
  this.mergeSort = mergeSort;
  }

// other function definitions go here

  function merge(left,right){
      var result = [];
```

```
    var leftLen = left.length;
    var rightLen = right.length;
    while (leftLen > 0 || rightLen > 0){
        if (leftLen > 0 && rightLen > 0){
    // Both A and B are still populated
            if (left[0] < right[0]){
                result.push(left.shift());
                leftLen -= 1;
            }
            else if (right[0] <= left[0]){
                result.push(right.shift());
                rightLen -= 1;
            }
        }
        else if (leftLen > 0){
            result.push(left.shift());
            leftLen -= 1;
        }
        else if (rightLen > 0){
            result.push(right.shift());
            rightLen -= 1;
        }
    }
    return result;
}

function mergeSort(array){
    var length = array.length;
    if (length <= 1){
    // This is the base case for the recursion
        return array;
    }
    var q = Math.floor(length/2);
    var left = mergeSort(array.slice(0,q));
    var right = mergeSort(array.slice(q));
    return merge(left, right);
    }
}
```

Testing the new addition provides the same output as previously displayed:

```
load ('./CArray.js');
var nums = new CArray(10);
nums.setData();
print('Start: ' + nums.toString());
nums.mergeSort();
print('Done: ' + nums.toString());
```

The Quicksort Algorithm

The Quicksort algorithm is one of the fastest sorting algorithms for large data sets. Quicksort is a divide-and-conquer algorithm that recursively breaks a list of data into successively smaller sublists consisting of the smaller elements and the larger elements. The algorithm continues this process until all the data in the list is sorted.

The algorithm divides the list into sublists by selecting one element of the list as a *pivot*. Data is sorted around the pivot by moving elements less than the pivot to the bottom of the list and elements that are greater than the pivot to the top of the list.

Figure 12-5 demonstrates how data is sorted around a pivot.

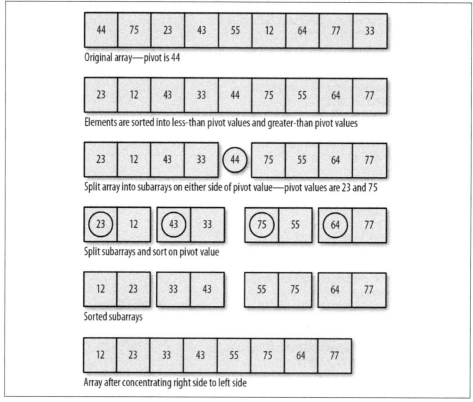

Figure 12-5. Sorting data around a pivot

Algorithm and pseudocode for the Quicksort algorithm

The algorithm for Quicksort is:

1. Pick a pivot element that divides the list into two sublists.
2. Reorder the list so that all elements less than the pivot element are placed before the pivot and all elements greater than the pivot are placed after it.

3. Repeat steps 1 and 2 on both the list with smaller elements and the list of larger elements.

This algorithm then translates into the following JavaScript program:

```javascript
function qSort(list) {
    if (list.length == 0) {
        return [];
    }
    var lesser = [];
    var greater = [];
    var pivot = list[0];
    for (var i = 1; i < list.length; i++) {
        if (list[i] < pivot) {
            lesser.push(list[i]);
        } else {
            greater.push(list[i]);
        }
    }
    return qSort(lesser).concat(pivot, qSort(greater));
}
```

The function first tests to see if the array has a length of 0. If so, then the array doesn't need sorting and the function returns. Otherwise, two arrays are created, one to hold the elements lesser than the pivot and the other to hold the elements greater than the pivot. The pivot is then selected by selecting the first element of the array. Next, the function loops over the array elements and places them in their proper array based on their value relative to the pivot value. The function is then called recursively on both the lesser array and the greater array. When the recursion is complete, the greater array is concatenated to the lesser array to form the sorted array and is returned from the function.

Let's test the algorithm with some data. Because our qSort program uses recursion, we won't use the array test bed; instead, we'll just create an array of random numbers and sort the array directly. The program is shown in Example 12-15.

Example 12-15. Sorting data with Quicksort

```javascript
function qSort(arr)
{
    if (arr.length == 0) {
        return [];
    }
    var left = [];
    var right = [];
    var pivot = arr[0];
    for (var i = 1; i < arr.length; i++) {

        if (arr[i] < pivot) {
```

```
            left.push(arr[i]);
        } else {

            right.push(arr[i]);
        }
    }
    return qSort(left).concat(pivot, qSort(right));
}
var a = [];
for (var i = 0; i < 10; ++i) {
    a[i] = Math.floor((Math.random()*100)+1);
}
print(a);
print();
print(qSort(a));
```

The output from this program is:

```
68,80,12,80,95,70,79,27,88,93

12,27,68,70,79,80,80,88,93,95
```

The Quicksort algorithm is best to use on large data sets; its performance degrades for smaller data sets.

To better demonstrate how Quicksort works, this next program highlights the pivot as it is chosen and how data is sorted around the pivot:

```
function qSort(arr)
{
    if (arr.length == 0) {
        return [];
    }
    var left = [];
    var right = [];
    var pivot = arr[0];
    for (var i = 1; i < arr.length; i++) {
        print("pivot: " + pivot + " current element: " + arr[i]);
        if (arr[i] < pivot) {
            print("moving " + arr[i] + " to the left");
            left.push(arr[i]);
        } else {
            print("moving " + arr[i] + " to the right");
            right.push(arr[i]);
        }
    }
    return qSort(left).concat(pivot, qSort(right));
}
var a = [];
for (var i = 0; i < 10; ++i) {
    a[i] = Math.floor((Math.random()*100)+1);
}
```

```
print(a);
print();
print(qSort(a));
```

The output from this program is:

```
9,3,93,9,65,94,50,90,12,65

pivot: 9 current element: 3
moving 3 to the left
pivot: 9 current element: 93
moving 93 to the right
pivot: 9 current element: 9
moving 9 to the right
pivot: 9 current element: 65
moving 65 to the right
pivot: 9 current element: 94
moving 94 to the right
pivot: 9 current element: 50
moving 50 to the right
pivot: 9 current element: 90
moving 90 to the right
pivot: 9 current element: 12
moving 12 to the right
pivot: 9 current element: 65
moving 65 to the right
pivot: 93 current element: 9
moving 9 to the left
pivot: 93 current element: 65
moving 65 to the left
pivot: 93 current element: 94
moving 94 to the right
pivot: 93 current element: 50
moving 50 to the left
pivot: 93 current element: 90
moving 90 to the left
pivot: 93 current element: 12
moving 12 to the left
pivot: 93 current element: 65
moving 65 to the left
pivot: 9 current element: 65
moving 65 to the right
pivot: 9 current element: 50
moving 50 to the right
pivot: 9 current element: 90
moving 90 to the right
pivot: 9 current element: 12
moving 12 to the right
pivot: 9 current element: 65
moving 65 to the right
pivot: 65 current element: 50
moving 50 to the left
pivot: 65 current element: 90
```

```
moving 90 to the right
pivot: 65 current element: 12
moving 12 to the left
pivot: 65 current element: 65
moving 65 to the right
pivot: 50 current element: 12
moving 12 to the left
pivot: 90 current element: 65
moving 65 to the left
3,9,9,12,50,65,65,90,93,94
```

Exercises

1. Run the three algorithms discussed in this chapter with string data rather than numeric data and compare the running times for the different algorithms. Are the results consistent with the results of using numeric data?

2. Create an array of 1,000 integers already sorted into numeric order. Write a program that runs each sorting algorithm with this array, timing each algorithm and comparing the times. How do these times compare to the times for sorting an array in random order?

3. Create an array of 1,000 integers sorted in reverse numerical order. Write a program that runs each sorting algorithm with this array, timing each algorithm, and compare the times.

4. Create an array of over 10,000 randomly generated integers and sort the array using both Quicksort and the JavaScript built-in sorting function, timing each function. Is there a time difference between the two functions?

CHAPTER 13

Searching Algorithms

Searching for data is a fundamental computer programming task that has been studied for many years. This chapter looks at just one aspect of the search problem—searching for a specified value in a list.

There are two ways to search for data in a list: *sequential search* and *binary search*. A sequential search is used when the items in a list are in random order; a binary search is used when the items in a list are in sorted order. Binary search is the more efficient algorithm, but you also have to take into account the extra time it takes to sort the data set before being able to search it for a value.

Commonly Used Functions in Examples

Two functions are commonly used in multiple examples in this chapter.

The first is `dispArr()`, which displays array contents, just as was used in Chapter 12.

```
function dispArr(arr) {
  for (var i = 0; i < arr.length; ++i) {
    putstr(arr[i] + " ");
    if (i % 10 == 9) {
      putstr("\n");
    }
  }
  if (i % 10 != 0) {
    putstr("\n");
  }
}
```

The second is `insertionsort()`, which preprocesses array entries, enabling more efficient searches.

```
function insertionsort(arr) {
    var temp, inner;
    for (var outer = 1; outer <= arr.length-1; ++outer) {
        temp = arr[outer];
        inner = outer;
        while (inner > 0 && (arr[inner-1] >= temp)) {
            arr[inner] = arr[inner-1];
            --inner;
        }
        arr[inner] = temp;
    }
}
```

Incorporate the code for either when called for in the example. === Sequential Search

The most obvious way to search for data in a list is to begin at the first element and move to each element in the list until you either find the data you are looking for or you reach the end of the list. This is called a sequential search, sometimes also called a *linear* search. It is an example of a *brute-force* search technique, where potentially every element in the data structure is visited on the way to a solution.

A sequential search is very easy to implement. Simply start a loop at the beginning of the list and compare each element to the data you are searching for. If you find a match, the search is over. If you get to the end of the list without generating a match, then the data searched for is not in the list.

Example 13-1 shows a function for performing sequential search on an array.

Example 13-1. The seqSearch() function

```
function seqSearch(arr, data) {
    for (var i = 0; i < arr.length; ++i) {
        if (arr[i] == data) {
            return true;
        }
    }
    return false;
}
```

If the data argument is found in the array, the function returns true immediately. If the function gets to the end of the array without finding a match, the function returns false.

Example 13-2 presents a program to test our sequential search function, including a function to make it easy to display the array's contents. As in Chapter 12, we use random number generation to populate an array with random numbers in the range of 1 to 100. We also use a function to display the contents of the array, just as we did in Chapter 12.

Example 13-2. Executing the seqSearch() function

```
var nums = [];
for (var i = 0; i < 100; ++i) {
   nums[i] = Math.floor(Math.random() * 101);
}
dispArr(nums);
putstr("Enter a number to search for: ");
var num = parseInt(readline());
print();
if (seqSearch(nums, num)) {
   print(num + " is in the array.");
}
else {
   print(num + " is not in the array.");
}
print();
dispArr(nums);
```

This program creates an array with random numbers in the range of 0 to 100. The user enters a value, the value is searched for, and the result is displayed. Finally, the program displays the complete array as proof of the validity of the function's return value. Here is a sample run of the program:

```
Enter a number to search for: 23

23 is in the array.

13 95 72 100 94 90 29 0 66 2 29
42 20 69 50 49 100 34 71 4 26
85 25 5 45 67 16 73 64 58 53
66 73 46 55 64 4 84 62 45 99
77 62 47 52 96 16 97 79 55 94
88 54 60 40 87 81 56 22 30 91
99 90 23 18 33 100 63 62 46 6
10 5 25 48 9 8 95 33 82 32
56 23 47 36 88 84 33 4 73 99
60 23 63 86 51 87 63 54 62
```

We can also write the sequential search function so that it returns the position where a match is found. Example 13-3 provides the definition of this new version of seq Search().

Example 13-3. Modifying the seqSearch() function to return the position found (or -1)

```
function seqSearch(arr, data) {
   for (var i = 0; i < arr.length; ++i) {
      if (arr[i] == data) {
         return i;
      }
   }
}
```

```
    return -1;
}
```

Notice that if the element searched for is not found, the function returns -1. This is the best value to return for the function since an array element cannot be stored in position -1.

Example 13-4 presents a program that uses this second definition of seqSearch().

Example 13-4. Testing the modified seqSearch() function

```
var nums = [];
for (var i = 0; i < 100; ++i) {
   nums[i] = Math.floor(Math.random() * 101);
}
putstr("Enter a number to search for: ");
var num = readline();
print();
var position = seqSearch(nums, num);
if (position > -1) {
   print(num + " is in the array at position " + position);
}
else {
   print(num + " is not in the array.");
}
print();
dispArr(nums);
```

Here is one run of the program:

```
Enter a number to search for: 22

22 is in the array at position 35

35 36 38 50 24 81 78 43 26 26 89
88 39 1 56 92 17 77 53 36 73
61 54 32 97 27 60 67 16 70 59
4 76 7 38 22 87 30 42 91 79
6 61 56 84 6 82 55 91 10 42
37 46 4 85 37 18 27 76 29 2
76 46 87 16 1 78 6 43 72 2
51 65 70 91 73 67 1 57 53 31
16 64 89 84 76 91 15 39 38 3
19 66 44 97 29 6 1 72 62
```

Keep in mind that the seqSearch() function is not as fast as the built-in Array.indexOf() function, but is shown here to demonstrate how search works.

Searching for Minimum and Maximum Values

Computer programming problems often involve searching for minimum and maximum values. In a sorted data structure, searching for these values is a trivial task. Searching an unsorted data structure, on the other hand, is a more challenging task.

Let's start by determining how we should search an array for a minimum value. Here is one algorithm:

1. Assign the first element of the array to a variable as the minimum value.

2. Begin looping through the array, starting with the second element, comparing each element with the current minimum value.

3. If the current element has a lesser value than the current minimum value, assign the current element as the new minimum value.

4. Move to the next element and repeat step 3.

5. The minimum value is stored in the variable when the program ends.

The operation of this algorithm is demonstrated in Figure 13-1.

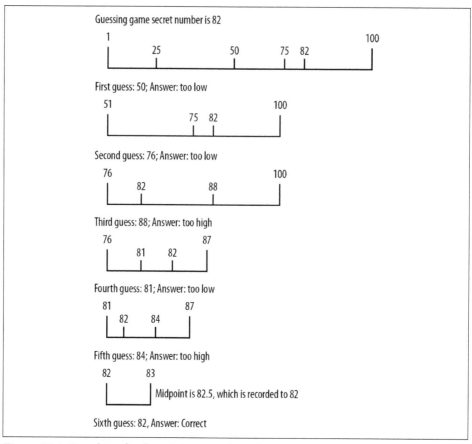

Figure 13-1. Searching for the minimum value of an array

This algorithm is easily transformed into a JavaScript function, as shown in Example 13-5.

Example 13-5. The findMin() function

```
function findMin(arr) {
   var min = arr[0];
   for (var i = 1; i < arr.length; ++i) {
      if (arr[i] < min) {
         min = arr[i];
      }
   }
   return min;
}
```

The key thing to notice about this function is that it begins with the second array element, since we are assigning the first array element as the current minimum value.

Let's test the function in a program, shown in Example 13-6. Note, you'll also want to add in the definition for dispArray(), shown in earlier examples.

Example 13-6. Finding the minimum value of an array

```
var nums = [];
for (var i = 0; i < 100; ++i) {
   nums[i] = Math.floor(Math.random() * 101);
}
var minValue = findMin(nums);
dispArr(nums);
print();
print("The minimum value is: " + minValue);
```

Here is the output from running this program:

```
89 30 25 32 72 70 51 42 25 24 53
55 78 50 13 40 48 32 26 2 14
33 45 72 56 44 21 88 27 68 15
93 98 73 28 16 46 87 28 65 38
67 16 85 63 23 69 64 91 9 70
81 27 97 82 6 88 3 7 46 13
11 64 31 26 38 28 13 17 69 90
1 6 7 64 43 9 73 80 98 46
27 22 87 49 83 6 39 42 51 54
84 34 53 78 40 14 5 76 62

The minimum value is: 1
```

The algorithm for finding the maximum value works in a similar fashion. We assign the first element of the array as the maximum value and then loop through the rest of the array, comparing each element to the current maximum value. If the current element is greater than the current maximum value, that element's value is stored in the variable. Example 13-7 shows the function definition.

Example 13-7. The findMax() function

```
function findMax(arr) {
   var max = arr[0];
   for (var i = 1; i < arr.length; ++i) {
      if (arr[i] > max) {
         max = arr[i];
      }
   }
   return max;
}
```

Example 13-8 shows a program that finds both the minimum value and the maximum value of an array.

Example 13-8. Using the `findMax()` function

```
var nums = [];
for (var i = 0; i < 100; ++i) {
    nums[i] = Math.floor(Math.random() * 101);
}
var minValue = findMin(nums);
dispArr(nums);
print();
print();
print("The minimum value is: " + minValue);
var maxValue = findMax(nums);
print();
print("The maximum value is: " + maxValue);
```

The output from this program is:

```
26 94 40 40 80 85 74 6 6 87 56
91 86 21 79 72 77 71 99 45 5
5 35 49 38 10 97 39 14 62 91
42 7 31 94 38 28 6 76 78 94
30 47 74 20 98 5 68 33 32 29
93 18 67 8 57 85 66 49 54 28
17 42 75 67 59 69 6 35 86 45
62 82 48 85 30 87 99 46 51 47
71 72 36 54 77 19 11 52 81 52
41 16 70 55 97 88 92 2 77

The minimum value is: 2

The maximum value is: 99
```

Using Self-Organizing Data

The fastest successful sequential searches on unordered data occur when the data being searched for is located at the beginning of the data set. You can ensure that a successfully found data item will be found quickly in the future by moving it to the beginning of a data set after it has been found in a search.

The concept behind this strategy is that we can minimize search times by locating items that are frequently searched for at the beginning of a data set. For example, if you are a librarian and you are asked several times a day for the same reference book, you will keep that book close to your desk for easy access. After many searches, the most frequently searched-for items will have moved from wherever they were stored to the beginning of the data set. This is an example of *self-organized data*: data that is organized not by the programmer before the program is executed, but by the program itself while the program is running.

It makes sense to allow your data to self-organize since the data being searched most likely follow the "80-20 rule," meaning that 80% of the searches made on a data set are searching for just 20% of the data in the set. Self-organization will eventually put that 20% at the beginning of the data set, where a simple sequential search will find them quickly.

Probability distributions such as the 80-20 rule are called Pareto distributions, named for Vilfredo Pareto, who discovered these distributions studying the spread of income and wealth in the late 19th century. See *The Art of Computer Programming: Volume 3, Sorting and Searching* by Donald Knuth (Addison-Wesley, 399-401) for more information on probability distributions in data sets.

We can modify our seqSearch() function to include self-organization fairly easily. Example 13-9 is our first attempt at the function definition.

Example 13-9. The seqSearch() function with self-organization

```
function seqSearch(arr, data) {
    for (var i = 0; i < arr.length; ++i) {
        if (arr[i] == data) {
            if (i > 0) {
                swap(arr,i,i-1);
            }
            return true;
        }
    }
    return false;
}
```

You'll notice that the function checks to make sure that the found data is not already in position 0.

The preceding definition uses a swap() function to exchange the found data with the data currently stored in the previous position. Here is the definition for the swap() function:

```
    function swap(arr, index, index1) {
        temp = arr[index];
        arr[index] = arr[index1];
        arr[index1] = temp;
    }
```

You'll notice that when using this technique, which is similar to how data is sorted with the bubble sort algorithm, the most frequently accessed elements will eventually work their way to the beginning of the data set. For example, this program:

```
var numbers = [5,1,7,4,2,10,9,3,6,8];
print(numbers);
for (var i = 1; i <= 3; i++) {
    seqSearch(numbers, 4);
    print(numbers);
}
```

generates the following output:

```
5,1,7,4,2,10,9,3,6,8
5,1,4,7,2,10,9,3,6,8
5,4,1,7,2,10,9,3,6,8
4,5,1,7,2,10,9,3,6,8
```

Notice how the value 4 "bubbles" up to the beginning of the list because it is being searched for three times in a row.

This technique also guarantees that if an element is already at the beginning of the data set, it won't get moved farther down.

Another way we can write the seqSearch() function with self-organizing data is to move a found item to the beginning of the data set, though we wouldn't want to exchange an element if it is already close to the beginning. To achieve this goal, we can swap found elements only if they are located at least some specified distance away from the beginning of the data set. We only have to determine what is considered to a be far enough away from the beginning of the data set to warrant moving the element closer to the beginning. Following the 80-20 rule again, we can make a rule that states that a data element is relocated to the beginning of the data set only if its location lies outside the first 20% of the items in the data set.

Example 13-10 shows the definition for this new version of seqSearch().

Example 13-10. seqSearch() with better self-organization

```
function seqSearch(arr, data) {
    for (var i = 0; i < arr.length; ++i) {
        if (arr[i] == data && i > (arr.length * 0.2)) {
            swap(arr,i,0);
            return true;
        }
        else if (arr[i] == data) {
            return true;
        }
    }
    return false;
}
```

Example 13-11 shows a program that tests this definition on a small data set of 10 elements. Again, copy the dispArr() and swap() functions from earlier.

Example 13-11. Searching with self-organization

```
var nums = [];
for (var i = 0; i < 10; ++i) {
   nums[i] = Math.floor(Math.random() * 11);
}
dispArr(nums);
print();
putstr("Enter a value to search for: ");
var val = parseInt(readline());
if (seqSearch(nums, val)) {
   print("Found element: ");
   print();
   dispArr(nums);
}
else {
   print(val + " is not in array.");
}
```

Here are the results of a sample run of this program:

```
4 5 1 8 10 1 3 10 0 1
Enter a value to search for: 3

Found element:

3 5 1 8 10 1 4 10 0 1
```

Let's run the program again and search for an element closer to the front of the data set:

```
4 2 9 5 0 6 9 4 5 6
Enter a value to search for: 2
Found element:

4 2 9 5 0 6 9 4 5 6
```

Because the searched-for element is so close to the front of the data set, the function does not change its position.

The searches we have discussed so far require that the data being searched be kept in an unordered sequence. However, we can speed up searches on large data sets significantly if we first sort the data set before performing a search. In the next section we discuss an algorithm for searching ordered data—the *binary search*.

Binary Search

When the data you are searching for are sorted, a more efficient search than the sequential search is the binary search. To understand how binary search works, imagine you are playing a number-guessing game where the possible number is between 1 and 100, and you have to guess the number as chosen by a friend. According to the rules, for every guess you make, your friend has three responses:

1. The guess is correct.
2. The guess is too high.
3. The guess is too low.

Following these rules, the best strategy is to choose the number 50 as your first guess. If that guess is too high, choose 25. If 50 is too low, you should guess 75. For each guess, you choose a midpoint by adjusting the lower range or the upper range of the numbers (depending on whether your guess is too low or too high). This midpoint becomes your new guess. As long as you follow this strategy, you will guess the correct number in the minimum possible number of guesses. Figure 13-2 demonstrates how this strategy works if the number to be guessed is 82.

We can implement this strategy as the binary search algorithm. This algorithm only works on a sorted data set. Here is the algorithm:

1. Set a lower bound to the first position of the array (0).
2. Set an upper bound to the last element of the array (length of array minus 1).
3. While the lower bound is less than or equal to the upper bound, do the following steps:
    a. Set the midpoint as (upper bound minus lower bound) divided by 2.
    b. If the midpoint element is less than the data being searched for, set a new lower bound to the midpoint plus 1.
    c. If the midpoint element is greater than the data being searched for, set a new upper bound to the midpoint minus 1.
    d. Otherwise, return the midpoint as the found element.

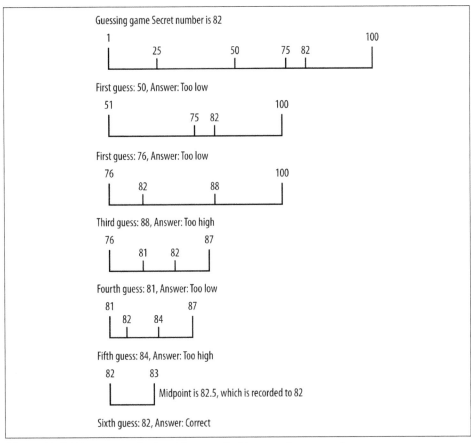

Figure 13-2. Binary search algorithm applied to guessing a number

Example 13-12 shows the JavaScript definition for the binary search algorithm, along with a program to test the definition. The dispArr() from earlier is also used.

Example 13-12. Using the binary search algorithm

```
function binSearch(arr, data) {
   var upperBound = arr.length-1;
   var lowerBound = 0;
   while (lowerBound <= upperBound) {
      var mid = Math.floor((upperBound + lowerBound) / 2);
      if (arr[mid] < data) {
         lowerBound = mid + 1;
      }
      else if (arr[mid] > data) {
         upperBound = mid - 1;
      }
      else {
```

```
        return mid;
      }
    }
    return -1;
}

function dispArr(arr) {
  for (var i = 0; i < arr.length; ++i) {
    putstr(arr[i] + " ");
    if (i % 10 == 9) {
       putstr("\n");
    }
  }
  if (i % 10 != 0) {
     putstr("\n");
  }
}

var nums = [];
for (var i = 0; i < 100; ++i) {
   nums[i] = Math.floor(Math.random() * 101);
}

insertionsort(nums);
dispArr(nums);
print();
putstr("Enter a value to search for: ");
var val = parseInt(readline());
var retVal = binSearch(nums, val);
if (retVal >= 0) {
   print("Found " + val + " at position " + retVal);
}
else {
   print(val + " is not in array.");
}
```

Here is the output from one run of the program:

```
1 2 3 5 6 6 6 6 7 7
7 9 9 12 14 17 17 20 21 22
25 26 26 26 29 29 33 36 37 37
37 37 37 39 39 40 41 41 42 43
43 44 44 45 45 45 45 46 46 47
47 47 48 49 51 51 58 60 60 61
61 63 63 64 64 65 67 71 72 74
74 74 76 77 77 78 79 80 80 80
82 82 83 84 85 85 85 85 86 86
87 88 91 91 91 94 95 96 99 100

Enter a value to search for: 72

Found 72 at position 68
```

It will be interesting to watch the function as it works its way through the search space looking for the value specified, so in Example 13-13, let's add a statement to the binSearch() function that displays the midpoint each time it is recalculated:

Example 13-13. binSearch() displaying the midpoint value

```
function binSearch(arr, data) {
    var upperBound = arr.length-1;
    var lowerBound = 0;
    while (lowerBound <= upperBound) {
        var mid = Math.floor((upperBound + lowerBound) / 2);
        print("Current midpoint: " + mid);
        if (arr[mid] < data) {
            lowerBound = mid + 1;
        }
        else if (arr[mid] > data) {
            upperBound = mid - 1;
        }
        else {
            return mid;
        }
    }
    return -1;
}
```

Now let's run the program again:

```
0 1 4 5 7 7 8 9 9 11
12 12 14 15 16 17 17 18 20 22
24 25 26 27 28 30 30 32 33 33
33 33 33 34 36 36 37 37 41 42
43 44 45 48 52 52 52 53 53 55
56 56 56 58 60 60 60 62 62 63
64 66 66 66 66 66 68 68 72 73
73 73 73 74 74 75 77 78 78 81
81 82 82 83 83 85 86 86 88 89
89 93 93 94 96 96 96 96 99 100

Enter a value to search for: 66
Current midpoint: 49
Current midpoint: 74
Current midpoint: 61
Found 66 at position 61
```

From this output, we see that the original midpoint value was 49. That's too low since we are searching for 82, so the next midpoint is calculated to be 74. That's still too low, so a new midpoint is calculated, 87, and that value holds the element we are searching for, so the search is over.

Counting Occurrences

When the binSearch() function finds a value, if there are other occurrences of the same value in the data set, the function will be positioned in the immediate vicinity of other like values. In other words, other occurrences of the same value will either be to the immediate left of the found value's position or to the immediate right of the found value's position.

If this fact isn't readily apparent to you, run the binSearch() function several times and take note of the position of the found value returned by the function. Here's an example of a sample run from earlier in this chapter:

```
0 1 2 3 5 7 7 8 8 9 10
11 11 13 13 13 14 14 14 15 15
18 18 19 19 19 19 20 20 20 21
22 22 22 23 23 24 25 26 26 29
31 31 33 37 37 37 38 38 43 44
44 45 48 48 49 51 52 53 53 58
59 60 61 61 62 63 64 65 68 69
70 72 72 74 75 77 77 79 79 79
83 83 84 84 86 86 86 91 92 93
93 93 94 95 96 96 97 98 100
Enter a value to search for: 37
Found 37 at position 45
```

If you count the position of each element, the number 37 found by the function is the one that is in the middle of the three occurrences of 37. This is just the nature of how the binSearch() function works.

So what does a function that counts the occurrences of values in a data set need to do to make sure that it counts all the occurrences? The easiest solution is to write two loops that move both down, or to the left of, the data set, counting occurrences, and up, or the right of, the data set, counting occurrences. Example 13-14 shows a definition of the count() function.

Example 13-14. The count() function

```
function count(arr, data) {
   var count = 0;
   var position = binSearch(arr, data);
   if (position > -1) {
      ++count;
      for (var i = position-1; i > 0; --i) {
         if (arr[i] == data) {
            ++count;
         }
         else {
            break;
         }
```

```
        }
        for (var i = position+1; i < arr.length; ++i) {
            if (arr[i] == data) {
                ++count;
            }
            else {
                break;
            }
        }
    }
    return count;
}
```

The function starts by calling the `binSearch()` function to search for the specified value. If the value is found in the data set, the the function begins counting occurrences by calling two `for` loops. The first loop works its way down the array, counting occurrences of the found value, stopping when the next value in the array doesn't match the found value. The second `for` loop works its way up the array, counting occurrences and stopping when the next value in the array doesn't match the found value.

Example 13-15 is the complete application demonstrating how to use `count()` and the other functions we've covered to this point.

Example 13-15. Using the count() function

```
function binSearch(arr, data) {
    var upperBound = arr.length-1;
    var lowerBound = 0;
    while (lowerBound <= upperBound) {
        var mid = Math.floor((upperBound + lowerBound) / 2);
        if (arr[mid] < data) {
            lowerBound = mid + 1;
        }
        else if (arr[mid] > data) {
            upperBound = mid - 1;
        }
        else {
            return mid;
        }
    }
    return -1;
}

function count(arr, data) {
    var count = 0;
    var position = binSearch(arr, data);
    if (position > -1) {
        ++count;
        for (var i = position-1; i > 0; --i) {
```

```
            if (arr[i] == data) {
                ++count;
            }
            else {
                break;
            }
        }
        for (var i = position+1; i < arr.length; ++i) {
            if (arr[i] == data) {
                ++count;
            }
            else {
                break;
            }
        }
    }
    return count;
}

function insertionsort(arr) {
    var temp, inner;
    for (var outer = 1; outer <= arr.length-1; ++outer) {
        temp = arr[outer];
        inner = outer;
        while (inner > 0 && (arr[inner-1] >= temp)) {
            arr[inner] = arr[inner-1];
            --inner;
        }
        arr[inner] = temp;
    }
}


function dispArr(arr) {
  for (var i = 0; i < arr.length; ++i) {
    putstr(arr[i] + " ");
    if (i % 10 == 9) {
        putstr("\n");
    }
  }
  if (i % 10 != 0) {
    putstr("\n");
  }
}


var nums = [];
for (var i = 0; i < 100; ++i) {
    nums[i] = Math.floor(Math.random() * 101);
}

insertionsort(nums);
```

```
dispArr(nums);
print();
putstr("Enter a value to count: ");
var val = parseInt(readline());
var retVal = count(nums, val);
print("Found " + retVal + " occurrences of " + val + ".");
```

Here is a sample run of the program:

```
 2  4  4  6  6  6  7  8  9 12
14 16 18 18 19 19 19 20 21 21
22 23 23 24 26 29 30 32 35 36
37 38 40 40 40 41 41 42 44 44
49 49 49 51 51 52 53 53 54 54
55 55 56 57 57 57 57 58 58 61
61 62 63 64 66 68 68 68 68 71
73 76 76 77 77 78 78 79 79 79
80 81 81 82 85 87 89 89 91 91
92 93 93 94 94 95 96 96 99 100

Enter a value to count: 58

Found 2 occurrences of 58.
```

Here is another sample run:

```
 0  0  0  1  2  3  4  5  9  9
10 11 11 11 11 13 13 15 16 17
18 19 20 21 21 23 23 26 28 29
29 32 33 34 35 35 36 37 37 37
38 40 40 41 41 42 44 44 46 47
47 47 48 48 50 51 53 54 56 57
60 62 62 65 65 67 69 69 70 74
74 75 75 77 78 79 79 81 82 83
86 88 88 88 88 89 89 89 89 89
90 90 91 91 92 92 97 97 98 99

Enter a value to count: 71

Found 0 occurrences of 71.
```

Searching Textual Data

Up to this point, all of our searches have been conducted on numeric data. We can also use the algorithms discussed in this chapter with textual data. First, let's define the data set we are using:

The nationalism of Hamilton was undemocratic. The democracy of Jefferson was, in the beginning, provincial. The historic mission of uniting nationalism and democracy was in the course of time given to new leaders from a region beyond the mountains, peopled by men and women from all sections and free from those state traditions which ran back to the early days of colonization. The voice

of the democratic nationalism nourished in the West was heard when Clay of
Kentucky advocated his American system of protection for industries; when
Jackson of Tennessee condemned nullification in a ringing proclamation that
has taken its place among the great American state papers; and when Lincoln
of Illinois, in a fateful hour, called upon a bewildered people to meet the
supreme test whether this was a nation destined to survive or to perish. And
it will be remembered that Lincoln's party chose for its banner that earlier
device--Republican--which Jefferson had made a sign of power. The "rail splitter"
from Illinois united the nationalism of Hamilton with the democracy of Jefferson,
and his appeal was clothed in the simple language of the people, not in the
sonorous rhetoric which Webster learned in the schools.

This paragraph of text was taken from the *big.txt* file found on Peter Norvig's website
(*http://www.norvig.com*). This file is stored as a text file (*.txt*) that is located in the
same directory as the JavaScript interpreter (*js.exe*).

To read the file into a program, we need just one line of code:

```
var words = read("words.txt").split(" ");
```

This line stores the text in an array by reading in the text from the file—
`read("words.txt")`—and then breaking up the file into words using the `split()`
function, which uses the space between each word as the delimiter. This code is not
perfect because puncuation is left in the file and is stored with the nearest word, but it
will suffice for our purposes.

Once the file is stored in an array, we can begin searching through the array to find
words. Let's begin with a sequential search and search for the word "rhetoric," which
is in the paragraph close to the end of the file. Let's also time the search so we can
compare it with a binary search. We covered timing code in Chapter 12 if you want to
go back and review that material. Example 13-16 shows the code.

Example 13-16. Searching a text file using seqSearch()

```
function seqSearch(arr, data) {
   for (var i = 0; i < arr.length; ++i) {
      if (arr[i] == data) {
         return i;
      }
   }
   return -1;
}

var words = read("words.txt").split(" ");
var word = "rhetoric";
var start = new Date().getTime();
var position = seqSearch(words, word);
var stop = new Date().getTime();
var elapsed = stop - start;
if (position >= 0) {
```

```
   print("Found " + word + " at position " + position + ".");
   print("Sequential search took " + elapsed + " milliseconds.");
}
else {
   print(word + " is not in the file.");
}
```

The output from this program is:

```
Found rhetoric at position 174.
Sequential search took 1 milliseconds.
```

Even though binary search is faster, we won't be able to measure any difference between seqSearch() and binSearch(), but we will run the program using binary search anyway to ensure that the binSearch() function works correctly with text. Example 13-17 shows the code and the output.

Example 13-17. Searching textual data with binSearch()

```
function binSearch(arr, data) {
   var upperBound = arr.length-1;
   var lowerBound = 0;
   while (lowerBound <= upperBound) {
      var mid = Math.floor((upperBound + lowerBound) / 2);
      if (arr[mid] < data) {
         lowerBound = mid + 1;
      }
      else if (arr[mid] > data) {
         upperBound = mid - 1;
      }
      else {
         return mid;
      }
   }
   return -1;
}

function insertionsort(arr) {
   var temp, inner;
   for (var outer = 1; outer <= arr.length-1; ++outer) {
      temp = arr[outer];
      inner = outer;
      while (inner > 0 && (arr[inner-1] >= temp)) {
         arr[inner] = arr[inner-1];
         --inner;
      }
      arr[inner] = temp;
   }
}

var words = read("words.txt").split(" ");
```

```
insertionsort(words);
var word = "rhetoric";
var start = new Date().getTime();
var position = binSearch(words, word);
var stop = new Date().getTime();
var elapsed = stop - start;
if (position >= 0) {
    print("Found " + word + " at position " + position + ".");
    print("Binary search took " + elapsed + " milliseconds.");
}
else {
    print(word + " is not in the file.");
}
```

The result of the application was:

```
Found rhetoric at position 125.
Binary search took 0 milliseconds.
```

In this age of superfast processors, it is harder and harder to measure the difference between sequential search and binary search on anything but the largest data sets. However, it has been proven mathematically that binary search is faster than sequential search on large data sets just due to the fact that the binary search algorithm eliminates half the search space (the elements of the array) with each iteration of the loop that controls the algorithm.

Exercises

1. The sequential search algorithm always finds the first occurrence of an element in a data set. Rewrite the algorithm so that the last occurrence of an element is returned.

2. Compare the time it takes to perform a sequential search with the total time it takes to both sort a data set using insertion sort and perform a binary search on the data set. What are your results?

3. Create a function that finds the second-smallest element in a data set. Can you generalize the function definition for the third-smallest, fourth-smallest, and so on? Test your functions with a data set of at least 1,000 elements. Test on both numbers and text.

CHAPTER 14

Advanced Algorithms

In this chapter we'll look at two advanced topics: dynamic programming and greedy algorithms. *Dynamic programming* is a technique that is sometimes considered the opposite of recursion. Where a recursive solution starts at the top and breaks the problem down, solving all small problems until the complete problem is solved, a dynamic programming solution starts at the bottom, solving small problems and combining them to form an overall solution to the big problem. This chapter departs from most of the other chapters in this book in that we don't really discuss an organizing data structure for working with these algorithms other than the array. Sometimes, a simple data structure is enough to solve a problem if the algorithm you are using is powerful enough.

A *greedy algorithm* is an algorithm that looks for "good solutions" as it works toward the complete solution. These good solutions, called *local optima*, will hopefully lead to the correct final solution, called the *global optimum*. The term "greedy" comes from the fact that these algorithms take whatever solution looks best at the time. Often, greedy algorithms are used when it is almost impossible to find a complete solution, owing to time and/or space considerations, and yet a suboptimal solution is acceptable.

A good source for more information on advanced algorithms and data structures is *Introduction to Algorithms* (MIT Press).

Dynamic Programming

Recursive solutions to problems are often elegant but inefficient. Many languages, including JavaScript, cannot efficiently translate recursive code to machine code, resulting in an inefficient though elegant computer program. This is not to say that using recursion is bad, per se, just that some imperative and object-oriented programming languages do not do a good job implementing recursion, since they do not feature recursion as a high-priority programming technique.

Many programming problems that have recursive solutions can be rewritten using the techniques of dynamic programming. A dynamic programming solution builds a table, usually using an array, that holds the results of the many subsolutions as the problem is broken down. When the algorithm is complete, the solution is found in a distinct spot in the table, as we'll see in the Fibonacci example next.

A Dynamic Programming Example: Computing Fibonacci Numbers

The Fibonacci numbers can be defined by the following sequence:

0, 1, 1, 2, 3, 5, 8, 13, 21, 34, 55, …

As you can tell, the sequence is generated by adding the previous two numbers in the sequence together. This sequence has a long history dating back to at least 700 AD and is named after the Italian mathematician Leornardo Fibonacci, who in 1202 used the sequence to describe the idealized growth of a rabbit population.

There is a simple recursive solution you can use to generate any specific number in the sequence. Here is the JavaScript code for a Fibonacci function:

```
function recurFib(n) {
    if (n < 2) {
        return n;
    }
    else {
        return recurFib(n-1) + recurFib(n-2);
    }
}

print(recurFib(10)); // displays 55
```

The problem with this function is that it is extremely inefficient. We can see exactly how inefficient it is by examining the recursion tree shown in Figure 14-1 for fib(5).

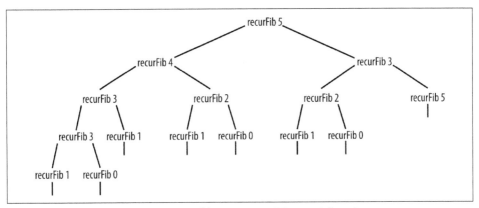

Figure 14-1. Recursion tree generated by recursive Fibonacci function

It is clear that too many values are recomputed during the recursive calls. If the compiler could keep track of the values that are already computed, the function would not be nearly so inefficient. We can design a much more efficient algorithm using dynamic programming techniques.

An algorithm designed using dynamic programming starts by solving the simplest subproblem it can solve, then using that solution to solve more complex subproblems until the entire problem is solved. The solutions to each subproblem are typically stored in an array for easy access.

We can demonstrate the essence of dynamic programming by examing the dynamic programming solution to computing Fibonacci numbers, as shown in the function definition in the following section:

```
function dynFib(n) {
    var val = [];
    for (var i = 0; i <= n; ++i) {
        val[i] = 0;
    }
    if (n == 1 || n == 2) {
        return 1;
    }
    else {
        val[1] = 1;
        val[2] = 2;
        for (var i = 3; i <= n; ++i) {
            val[i] = val[i-1] + val[i-2];
        }
        return val[n-1];
    }
}
```

The val array is where we store intermediate results. The first part of the if statement returns the value 1 if the Fibonacci number to be computed is 1 or 2. Otherwise, the values 1 and 2 are stored in positions 1 and 2 of val. The for loop runs from 3 to the input argument, assigning each array element the sum of the previous two array elements, and when the loop is complete, the last value in the array will be the last computed Fibonacci number, which is the number asked for and is the value returned by the function.

The arrangement of the Fibonacci sequence in the val array is shown here:

val[0] = 0 val[1] = 1 val[2] = 2 val[3] = 3 val[4] = 5 val[5] = 8 val[6] = 13

Let's compare the time it takes to compute a Fibonacci number using both the recursive function and the dynamic programming function. Example 14-1 lists the code for the timing test.

Example 14-1. Timing test for recursive and dynamic programming versions of Fibonacci function

```
function recurFib(n) {
   if (n < 2) {
      return n;
   }
   else {
      return recurFib(n-1) + recurFib(n-2);
   }
}

function dynFib(n) {
   var val = [];
   for (var i = 0; i <= n; ++i) {
      val[i] = 0;
   }
   if (n == 1 || n == 2) {
      return 1;
   }
   else {
      val[1] = 1;
      val[2] = 2;
      for (var i = 3; i <= n; ++i) {
         val[i] = val[i-1] + val[i-2];
      }
      return val[n-1];
   }
}

var start = new Date().getTime();
print(recurFib(10));
var stop = new Date().getTime();
print("recursive time - " + (stop-start) + "milliseconds");
print();
start = new Date().getTime();
print(dynFib(10));
```

```
stop = new Date().getTime();
print("dynamic programming time - " + (stop-start) + " milliseconds");
```

The output from this program is:

```
55
recursive time - 0 milliseconds

55
dynamic programming time - 0 milliseconds
```

If we run the program again, this time computing fib(20), we get:

```
6765
recursive time - 2 milliseconds

6765
dynamic programming time - 0 milliseconds
```

Finally, we compute fib(30) and we get:

```
832040
recursive time - 42 milliseconds

832040
dynamic programming time - 0 milliseconds
```

Clearly, the dynamic programming solution is much more efficient than the recursive solution when we compute anything over fib(20).

Finally, you may have already figured out that it's not necessary to use an array when computing a Fibonacci number using the iterative solution. The array was used because dynamic programming algorithms usually store intermediate results in an array. Here is the definition of an iterative Fibonacci function that doesn't use an array:

```
function iterFib(n) {
    var last = 1;
    var nextLast = 1;
    var result = 1;
    for (var i = 2; i < n; ++i) {
        result = last + nextLast;
        nextLast = last;
        last = result;
    }
    return result;
}
```

This version of the function will compute Fibonacci numbers as efficiently as the dynamic programming version.

Finding the Longest Common Substring

Another problem that lends itself to a dynamic programming solution is finding the longest common substring in two strings. For example, in the words "raven" and "havoc," the longest common substring is "av." A common use of finding the longest common substring is in genetics, where DNA molecules are described using the first letter of the nucleobase of a nucleotide.

We'll start with the brute-force solution to this problem. Given two strings, A and B, we can find the longest common substring by starting at the first character of A and comparing each character to the corresponding character of B. When a nonmatch is found, move to the second character of A and start over with the first character of B, and so on.

There is a better solution using dynamic programming. The algorithm uses a two-dimensional array to store the results of comparisons of the characters in the same position in the two strings. Initially, each element of the array is set to 0. Each time a match is found in the same position of the two arrays, the element at the corresponding row and column of the array is incremented by 1; otherwise the element stays set to 0. Along the way, a variable is keeping track of how many matches are found. This variable, along with an indexing variable, are used to retrieve the longest common substring once the algorithm is finished.

Example 14-2 presents the complete definition of the algorithm. After the code, we'll explain how it works.

Example 14-2. A function for determining the longest common substring of two strings

```
function lcs(word1, word2) {
    var max = 0;
    var index = 0;
    var lcsarr = new Array(word1.length+1);
    for (var i = 0; i <= word1.length+1; ++i) {
        lcsarr[i] = new Array(word2.length+1);
        for (var j = 0; j <= word2.length+1; ++j) {
            lcsarr[i][j] = 0;
        }
    }
    for (var i = 0; i <= word1.length; ++i) {
        for (var j = 0; j <= word2.length; ++j) {
            if (i == 0 || j == 0) {
                lcsarr[i][j] = 0;
            }
            else {
                if (word1[i-1] == word2[j-1]) {
                    lcsarr[i][j] = lcsarr[i-1][j-1] + 1;
                }
                else {
```

```
            lcsarr[i][j] = 0;
        }
    }
    if (max < lcsarr[i][j]) {
        max = lcsarr[i][j];
        index = i;
    }
  }
 }
 var str = "";
 if (max == 0) {
    return "";
 }
 else {
    for (var i = index-max; i <= max; ++i) {
        str += word2[i];
    }
    return str;
 }
}
```

The first section of the function sets up a couple of variables and the two-dimensional array. Most languages have a simple declaration for two-dimensional arrays, but Java-Script makes you jump through a few hoops by declaring an array inside an array. The last for loop in the code fragment initializes the array. Here's the first section:

```
function lcs(word1, word2) {
    var max = 0;
    var index = 0;
    var lcsarr = new Array(word1.length+1);
    for (var i = 0; i <= word1.length+1; ++i) {
        lcsarr[i] = new Array(word2.length+1);
        for (var j = 0; j <= word2.length+1; ++j) {
            lcsarr[i][j] = 0;
        }
    }
```

Now here is the code for the second section of the function:

```
for (var i = 0; i <= word1.length; ++i) {
    for (var j = 0; j <= word2.length; ++j) {
        if (i == 0 || j == 0) {
            lcsarr[i][j] = 0;
        }
        else {
            if (word1[i-1] == word2[j-1]) {
                lcsarr[i][j] = lcsarr[i-1][j-1] + 1;
            }
            else {
                lcsarr[i][j] = 0;
            }
        }
```

```
        if (max < lcsarr[i][j]) {
            max = lcsarr[i][j];
            index = i;
        }
    }
}
```

The second section builds the table that keeps track of character matches. The first elements of the array are always set to 0. Then if the corresponding characters of the two strings match, the current array element is set to 1 plus the value stored in the previous array element. For example, if the two strings are "back" and "cace," and the algorithm is on the second character, then a 1 is placed in the current element, since the previous element wasn't a match and a 0 is stored in that element (0 + 1). The algorithm then moves to the next position, and since it also matches for both strings, a 2 is placed in the current array element (1 + 1). The last characters of the two strings don't match, so the longest common substring is 2. Finally, if max is less than the value now stored in the current array element, it is assigned the value of the current array element, and index is set to the current value of i. These two variables will be used in the last section to determine where to start retrieving the longest common substring.

For example, given the two strings "abbcc" and "dbbcc," here is the state of the lcsarr array as the algorithm progresses:

```
0 0 0 0 0
0 0 0 0 0
0 1 1 0 0
0 1 2 0 0
0 0 0 3 1
0 0 0 1 4
```

The last section builds the longest common substring by determining where to start. The value of index minus max is the starting point, and the value of max is the stopping point:

```
var str = "";
if (max == 0) {
    return "";
}
else {
    for (var i = index-max; i <= max; ++i) {
        str += word2[i];
    }
    return str;
}
```

Given again the two strings "abbcc" and "dbbcc," the program returns "bbcc."

The Knapsack Problem: A Recursive Solution

A classic problem in the study of algorithms is the knapsack problem. Imagine you are a safecracker and you break open a safe filled with all sorts of treasure, but all you have to carry the loot is a small backpack. The items in the safe differ in both size and value. You want to maximize your take by filling the backpack with those items that are worth the most.

There is, of course, a brute-force solution to this problem, but the dynamic programming solution is more efficient. The key idea to solving the knapsack problem with a dynamic programming solution is to calculate the maximum value for every item up to the total capacity of the knapsack.

If the safe in our example has five items, the items have a size of 3, 4, 7, 8, and 9, respectively, and values of 4, 5, 10, 11, and 13, respectively, and the knapsack has a capacity of 16, then the proper solution is to pick items 3 and 5 with a total size of 16 and a total value of 23.

The code for solving this problem is quite short, but it won't make much sense without the context of the whole program, so let's take a look at the program to solve the knapsack problem. Our solution uses a recursive function:

```
function max(a, b) {
   return (a > b) ? a : b;
}

function knapsack(capacity, size, value, n) {
   if (n == 0 || capacity == 0) {
      return 0;
   }
   if (size[n-1] > capacity) {
      return knapsack(capacity, size, value, n-1);
   }
   else {
      return max(value[n-1] +
               knapsack(capacity-size[n-1], size, value, n-1),
               knapsack(capacity, size, value, n-1));
   }
}

var value = [4,5,10,11,13];
var size = [3,4,7,8,9];
var capacity = 16;
var n = 5;
print(knapsack(capacity, size, value, n));
```

The output from this program is:

```
23
```

The problem with this recursive solution to the knapsack problem is that, because it is recursive, many subproblems are revisited during the course of the recursion. A better solution to the knapsack problem is to use a dynamic programming technique to solve the problem, as shown below.

The Knapsack Problem: A Dynamic Programming Solution

Whenever we find a recursive solution to a problem, we can usually rewrite the solution using a dynamic programming technique and end up with a more efficient program. The knapsack problem can definitely be rewritten in a dynamic programming manner. All we have to do is use an array to store temporary solutions until we get to the final solution.

The following program demonstrates how the knapsack problem we encountered earlier can be solved using dynamic programming. The optimum value for the given constraints is, again, 23. Example 14-3 shows the code.

Example 14-3. A dynamic programming solution to the knapsack problem

```
function max(a, b) {
   return (a > b) ? a : b;
}

function dKnapsack(capacity, size, value, n) {
   var K = [];
   for (var i = 0; i <= capacity+1; i++) {
      K[i] = [];
   }
   for (var i = 0; i <= n; i++) {
      for (var w = 0; w <= capacity; w++) {
         if (i == 0 || w == 0) {
            K[i][w] = 0;
         }
         else if (size[i-1] <= w) {
            K[i][w] = max(value[i-1] + K[i-1][w-size[i-1]],
                          K[i-1][w]);
         }
         else {
            K[i][w] = K[i-1][w];
         }
         putstr(K[i][w] + " ");
      }
      print();
   }

   return K[n][capacity];
}

var value = [4,5,10,11,13];
```

```
var size = [3,4,7,8,9];
var capacity = 16;
var n = 5;
print(dKnapsack(capacity, size, value, n));
```

As the program runs, it displays the values being stored in the table as the algorithm works toward a solution. Here is the output:

```
0 0 0 0 0 0 0 0 0 0 0 0 0 0 0 0 0
0 0 0 4 4 4 4 4 4 4 4 4 4 4 4 4 4
0 0 0 4 5 5 5 9 9 9 9 9 9 9 9 9 9
0 0 0 4 5 5 5 10 10 10 14 15 15 15 19 19 19
0 0 0 4 5 5 5 10 11 11 14 15 16 16 19 21 21
0 0 0 4 5 5 5 10 11 13 14 15 17 18 19 21 23
23
```

The optimal solution to the problem is found in the last cell of the two-dimensional table, which is found in the bottom-right corner of the table. You will also notice that using this technique does not tell you which items to pick to maximize output, but from inspection, the solution is to pick items 3 and 5, since the capacity is 16, item 3 has a size 7 (value 10), and item 5 has a size 9 (value 13).

Greedy Algorithms

In the previous sections, we examined dynamic programming algorithms that can be used to optimize solutions that are found using a suboptimal algorithm—solutions that are often based on recursion. For many problems, resorting to dynamic programming is overkill and a simpler algorithm will suffice.

One example of a simpler algorithm is the *greedy* algorithm. A greedy algorithm is one that always chooses the best solution at the time, with no regard to how that choice will affect future choices. Using a greedy algorithm generally indicates that the implementer hopes that the series of "best" local choices made will lead to a final "best" choice. If so, then the algorithm has produced an optimal solution; if not, a suboptimal solution has been found. However, for many problems, it is just not worth the trouble to find an optimal solution, so using a greedy algorithm works just fine.

A First Greedy Algorithm Example: The Coin-Changing Problem

A classic example of following a greedy algorithm is making change. Let's say you buy some items at the store and the change from your purchase is 63 cents. How does the clerk determine the change to give you? If the clerk follows a greedy algorithm, he or she gives you two quarters, a dime, and three pennies. That is the smallest number of coins that will equal 63 cents without using half-dollars.

Example 14-4 demonstrates a program that uses a greedy algorithm to make change (under the assumption that the amount of change is less than one dollar).

Example 14-4. A greedy algorithm for solving the coin-changing problem

```
function makeChange(origAmt, coins) {
    var remainAmt = 0;
    if (origAmt % .25 < origAmt) {
        coins[3] = parseInt(origAmt / .25);
        remainAmt = origAmt % .25;
        origAmt = remainAmt;
    }
    if (origAmt % .1 < origAmt) {
        coins[2] = parseInt(origAmt / .1);
        remainAmt = origAmt % .1;
        origAmt = remainAmt;
    }
    if (origAmt % .05 < origAmt) {
        coins[1] = parseInt(origAmt / .05);
        remainAmt = origAmt % .05;
        origAmt = remainAmt;
    }
    coins[0] = parseInt(origAmt / .01);
}

function showChange(coins) {
    if (coins[3] > 0) {
        print("Number of quarters - " + coins[3] + " - " + coins[3] * .25);
    }
    if (coins[2] > 0) {
        print("Number of dimes - " + coins[2] + " - " + coins[2] * .10);
    }
    if (coins[1] > 0) {
        print("Number of nickels - " + coins[1] + " - " + coins[1] * .05);
    }
    if (coins[0] > 0) {
        print("Number of pennies - " + coins[0] + " - " + coins[0] * .01);
    }
}

var origAmt = .63;
var coins = [];
makeChange(origAmt, coins);
showChange(coins);
```

The output from this program is:

```
Number of quarters - 2 - 0.5
Number of dimes - 1 - 0.1
Number of pennies - 3 - 0.03
```

The makeChange() function starts with the highest denomination, quarters, and tries to make as much change with them as possible. The total number of quarters is stored in the coins array. Once the amount left becomes less than a quarter, the algorithm moves to dimes, making as much change with dimes as possible. The total number of dimes is then stored in the coins array. The algorithm then moves to nickels and pennies in the same manner.

This solution always finds the optimal solution as long as the normal coin denominations are used and all the possible denominations are available. Not being able to use one particular denomination, such as nickels, can lead to a suboptimal solution.

A Greedy Algorithm Solution to the Knapsack Problem

Earlier in this chapter we examined the knapsack problem and provided both recursive and dynamic programming solutions for it. In this section, we'll examine how we can implement a greedy algorithm to solve this problem.

A greedy algorithm can be used to solve the knapsack problem if the items we are placing in the knapsack are continuous in nature. In other words, the items must be things that cannot be counted discretely, such as cloth or gold dust. If we are using continous items, we can simply divide the unit price by the unit volume to determine the value of the item. An optimal solution in this case is to place as much of the item with the highest value into the knapsack as possible until the item is depleted or the knapsack is full, followed by as much of the second-highest-value item as possible, and so on. The reason we can't find an optimal greedy solution using discrete items is because we can't put "half a television" into a knapsack. Discrete knapsack problems are known as 0-1 problems because you must take either all or none of an item.

This type of knapsack problem is called a fractional knapsack problem. Here is the algorithm for solving fractional knapsack problems:

1. Knapsack has a capacity W and items have values V and weights w.
2. Rank items by v/w ratio.
3. Consider items in terms of decreasing ratio.
4. Take as much of each item as possible.

Table 14-1 gives the weights, values, and ratios for four items.

Table 14-1. Fractional knapsack items

Item	A	B	C	D
Value	50	140	60	60
Size	5	20	10	12

Item	A	B	C	D
Ratio	10	7	6	5

Given the table above, and assuming that the knapsack being used has a capacity of 30, the optimal solution for the knapsack problem is to take all of item A, all of item B, and half of item C. This combination of items will result in a value of 220.

The code for finding the optimal solution to this knapsack problem is shown below:

```
function ksack(values, weights, capacity) {
    var load = 0;
    var i = 0;
    var w = 0;
    while (load < capacity && i < 4) {
        if (weights[i] <= (capacity-load)) {
            w += values[i];
            load += weights[i];
        }
        else {
            var r = (capacity-load)/weights[i];
            w += r * values[i];
            load += weights[i];
        }
        ++i;
    }
    return w;
}

var items = ["A", "B", "C", "D"];
var values = [50, 140, 60, 60];
var weights = [5, 20, 10, 12];
var capacity = 30;
print(ksack(values, weights, capacity)); // displays 220
```

Exercises

1. Write a program that uses a brute-force technique to find the longest common substring.

2. Write a program that allows the user to change the constraints of a knapsack problem in order to explore how changing the constraints will change the results of the solution. For example, you can change the capacity of the knapsack, the values of the items, or the weights of the items. It is probably a good idea to change only one of these constraints at a time.

3. Using the greedy algorithm technique for coin changing, but not allowing the algorithm to use dimes, find the solution for 30 cents. Is this solution optimal?

Index

K

key value, 129
key-value pairs, 95
keys() function, 100
knapsack problem
    dynamic programming solution, 222
    greedy algorithm solution, 225
    recursive solution, 221

L

last-in, first-out (LIFO) data structures, 53
lastIndexOf() function, 20
leaf nodes, 128
    removing from binary search tree, 139
left nodes, 130
length property
    arrays, 16, 17
    lists, 37
    queues, 64
    stacks, 54
    string keys in dictionaries and, 97
    using push() instead of to extend arrays, 22
length() function
    returning number of elements in list, 40
    Stack class, 55
levels (in trees), 129
linear probing, 116
linear search, 192
    (see also sequential search)
linked lists, xi, 79-93, 79
    circularly linked, 91
    defined, 80
    doubly linked, 87-91
        displaying elements in reverse order, 88
        LList class as doubly linked list, 89
    head node, 80
    inserting and removing nodes, 80
    object-based design, 81-87
        complete code for Node class and LList
            class, 85
        inserting nodes, 82
        linked list class (LList), 81
        LList class and test program, 83
        Node class, 81
        removing nodes, 84
    other functions for, 92
    using instead of arrays, 79
links, 80
List class, 39-45

append() function, 39
clear() function, 42
contains() function, 42
finding element in a list, 40
insert() function, 41
length() function, 40
remove() function, 40
    find() helper function, 40
lists, 37-51
    abstract data type (ADT), 37
    building a list-based application, 45-51
        managing a video rental kiosk, 47-50
        reading text files, 45
    iterating through, 44
listSize property, 37
    decrementing after removing list element,
        40
    incrementing after appending list element,
        39
local scope, 9
loops, 7
    in graphs, 146

M

map() function, 28
Math class
    floor() function, 165
    random() function, 165
math functions, examples of use, 3
math library, 3
maximum value, searching for, 136, 197
members (of sets), 119
Mergesort algorithm, 181-185
    bottom-up, 181
    JavaScript implementation of bottom-up
        Mergesort, 183
        adding mergeSort() and mergeArrays()
            to CArray class, 184
    top-down, 181
minimum value, searching for, 136, 195
modular hashing, 105
Mozilla Developer Network website, 22
multidimensional arrays, 30, 114

N

next property, Node class, 81
Nightly Build web page, 1
Node class, 81, 85
    defining for binary search tree, 130

R

radix sort, 71
    implementing using queues, 72-74
random numbers, 110
random() function, Math class, 165
read() function, 46, 210
real-world systems modeled by graphs, 147
recursion, 10
    demonstrating with Stack class, 60
reduce() function, 27
reduceRight() function, 28
remove() function
    Dictionary class, 96
    for doubly linked list, 87
    List class, 40
    removing nodes from binary search tree,
        139
    removing nodes from linked list, 84
    Set class, 121
removeNode() function, binary search tree, 139
repetition constructs, 7
right nodes, 130
root node, 128

S

scope, 8
searches, binary search tree, 135-138
    for minimim and maximum value, 136
    for specific value, 137
searching, xi
searching algorithms, 191-212
    binary search, 201-212
    sequential search, 192-201
searching graphs, 150-154
    breadth-first search, 152
        leading to shortest paths, 154
    depth-first search, 150
Sedgewick, Robert, 178
selection sort, 169
    selectionSort() function, 170
self-organized data, 198
separate chaining, 113
sequential search, 192-201
    executing seqSearch() function, 192
    modifying seqSearch() to return position
        found, 193
    performing on array with seqSearch() funci-
        ton, 192
    program testing modified seqSearch(), 194

searching a text file, 210
searching for minimum and maximum val-
    ues, 195
using self-organizing data, 198
sets, xi, 119-126
    definitions of terms, 119
    operations performed on, 120
    Set class implementation, 120
        add() function, 120
        difference() function, 125
        intersect() function, 123
        more set operations, 122
        remove() function, 121
        subset() function, 124
        union() function, 123
shallow copies, 18
Shell, Donald, 175
Shellsort algorithm, 175-180
    comparing array before and after sorting,
        177
    comparing efficiency of shellsort() func-
        tions, 180
    gap sequence, 175, 178
        adding to CArray class definition, 176
    running shellsort() on small data set, 177
    shellsort() function, adding to CArray class,
        176
    using larger gap sequence and larger data
        set, 178
shift() function, 23
    removing element from front of an array, 64
shortest-path algorithm, 154
show() function, 92
    Node class in binary search tree, 130
showAll() function, Dictionary class, 96, 100
showDistro() function, HashTable class, 105
showGraph() function, Graph class, 149, 159
simple cycles, 146
simpleHash() function, 105, 106
    adding print() statement to, 106
    collisions, 107
    hashing integer keys, 110
size() function, using with sets, 124
some() function, 26
sort() function
    Dictionary class, 100
    sorting strings, 24
    using to order numbers, 25
sorting, xi

V

value-returning functions, defining, 8
var keyword
    in variable declarations, 3
    leaving off when defining variables, 9
variables
    declaring and initializing, 3
    global, 9
    scope, 8
vertices, 145
    strongly connected, 146
void functions, 7

W

while loop, 7

About the Author

Michael McMillan is an instructor of computer information systems at Pulaski Technical College in North Little Rock, Arkansas. He is also an ajunct instructor of information science at the University of Arkansas at Little Rock. Before moving to academia, he was a programmer/analyst for Arkansas Children's Hospital, where he worked in statistical computing and data analysis.

Colophon

The animal on the cover of *Data Structures and Algorithms with JavaScript* is an Amur hedgehog (*Erinaceus amurensis*), also known as the Chinese hedgehog. This species is 1 out of 14 that can be found worldwide today, and is native to Amur Krai and Primorye in Russia, Manchuria in China, and the Korean Peninsula. Like most hedgehogs, the Chinese hedgehog prefers tall grasses and undergrowth. In the wild, they feed on worms, centipedges, insects, mice, snails, frogs, and snakes. Named for the distinct noise made as they forage for food, they hunt primarily using their senses of smell and hearing. Their sniff often resembles a pig-like grunt.

The Amur hedgehog weighs an average of 1.3 to 2.2 pounds and measures between 5.5 to 12 inches in length, its tail measuring around 1-2 of those inches. As a deterrent to predators (such as birds or wild dogs), the hedgehogs are covered in short, smooth spines. If threatened, the hedgehog rolls up into a ball, leaving only the spines exposed; this is also the position in which the hedgehog sleeps, usually in cool dark depressions or holes.

Hedgehogs are solitary animals, not often socializing with other hedgehogs even when encountered while out foraging for food. The only time hedgehogs socialize is during mating season, after which they go their separate ways, leaving the female hedgehog to raise any young that were conceived. Females are very protective of their young; male hedgehogs have been known to eat their young.

The cover image is from source unknown. The cover fonts are URW Typewriter and Guardian Sans. The text font is Adobe Minion Pro; the heading font is Adobe Myriad Condensed; and the code font is Dalton Maag's Ubuntu Mono.

Learn from experts.
Find the answers you need.

Sign up for a **10-day free trial** to get **unlimited access** to all of the content on Safari, including Learning Paths, interactive tutorials, and curated playlists that draw from thousands of ebooks and training videos on a wide range of topics, including data, design, DevOps, management, business—and much more.

Start your free trial at:

oreilly.com/safari

(No credit card required)

Milton Keynes UK
Ingram Content Group UK Ltd.
UKHW051427210524
442884UK00021B/520